MIDLIFE

Awakening

Verena
Enjoy the next
chapter of
your life!

Cathy
Derksen

20 Women Share Inspiring Stories
of Midlife Transformation

MIDLIFE
Awakening

20 Women Share Inspiring Stories
of Midlife Transformation

Dedications

For my mom and all women of any age who wrestle the chains of societal expectations while looking for some fun.

~Beth Jaffe

I dedicate my chapter and this book to all of the women around the world who are facing the challenges of transformation through midlife. As a community, we will lift each other and the world to higher a place of peace, freedom and success.

~Cathy Derksen

Ryan, for your complete, unconditional support and being my biggest encourager – always seeing my potential bigger than I imagine and celebrating my successes.

~Kay McBreairty

This chapter of my life is dedicated to my long-missed mother EfatSadat and my caring father, Aliakbar, for instilling in me the love for mysticism, poetry, and great literature, and celebrating my creative adventures.

~Nahid Boustani

I dedicate my chapter to all the people who put stones in my way. I am building stairs with them. Thank you for making me who I am today.

~Simone Bosman

Table of Contents

Introduction

I would like to congratulate this team of authors for creating such an inspiring collection of stories, tools and strategies. I am proud to have conceived and curated this amazing anthology. I'm honoured to have this opportunity to share these women's stories with the world.

The intention of this book is to inspire the reader to take on midlife as the opening of an exciting new chapter in life. Coming together as a community to share our wisdom, experiences and vision for the future is my favorite way to support each other on this journey. As a community, we can create a ripple effect of positive change in the world.

The authors in this book come from many countries around the world and they each bring to this book their own perspective and acquired wisdom. I hope these stories inspire you to take on a bigger vision for your life and to discover a community of support to lift you along the way.

Cathy Derksen

CHAPTER 1

Open to a World of Possibilities

by Cathy Derksen

---

*Although we're the most educated, powerful generations
of women in history... studies are showing that we're less
happy, and more lonely and depressed than we've ever
been.* ~ Dr. Claire Zammit

When I first heard this quote, I was shocked. How could it be
that we, as women in the 21st century, have come so far in
establishing our rights and improving equity, but we are feeling so
disconnected and alone? Dr. Zammit's work sheds light on many issues
that are challenging women today and her teachings have been a major
factor in my own personal growth.

Looking back over my own life, I see how I fit into this pattern
without even realizing it. For the first four decades of my life, I followed
the rules and the road map that society had set out for me. I graduated

university and found a great career with benefits and a pension. I got married and had a house in the burbs, two cars, two kids and a dog. I was checking all the boxes, but I had not really stopped to think about my own vision of who I was or how I wanted to create value in my own life. I spent years going through the motions of what I thought life was supposed to be. In the process, I had completely lost touch with myself. At one point, I remember realizing I didn't even know what kind of food or music I liked. I was numb to my own emotions and needs.

After years of tolerating an emotionally abusive marriage and a toxic work environment, something inside me started to shift and awaken. I was experiencing an expanding knowledge that there was more to life than this. I started to become aware of a growing internal sense that I needed to do more with my life. My eyes started to open to the vast opportunities that were available to me.

Reflecting back now, I see how I fit into the reality that Dr Zammit describes in the earlier quote. I had all of the things and had checked off all of the boxes, but I was feeling empty and alone in my life. I felt a calling and a yearning for something different, but I had no idea what that would look like. My midlife awakening had begun.

Fast forward over a decade and I find myself in an entirely different reality. It has been a journey filled with challenges and triumphs, pivots, and opportunities. I've embraced a model of lifelong learning and personal growth. Since leaving my abusive marriage and stepping into a completely different career, I have allowed myself to create a new vision of my future.

I've learned so much along the way and I've followed my intuition to a new life that gives me the space to not only continue my journey of personal growth, but also support other women to step into a life that fills them with joy and inspiration. Together we are shifting the trend away from frustration, loneliness, and depression. As a community, we are lifting each other into a brighter future.

Step into Midlife, Bold and Brilliant

This quote has become a focal point for my work:

Don't ask what the world needs. Ask yourself what makes you come alive, then go do that! Because, what the world needs is people who have come alive!
~ Howard Thurman

As I followed my intuition and allowed myself to awaken to new opportunities and approaches to life, I discovered what makes me come alive. I discovered my calling to support other women as they stepped into their own midlife awakening. In my experience, many of us do not give ourselves permission to even think about our own needs and dreams. We have spent so many years looking after everyone else and following the path we were on, we lost track of our bigger vision for ourselves.

What is it that makes you come alive? What makes you feel energized?

As we move into our 50s, 60s, and 70s, this is the time to re-evaluate our priorities and allow ourselves to visualize a life that fills us with connection and fulfillment. Society has been telling us that women in midlife should slow down and expect less from life. These limiting beliefs and expectations need to be challenged and tossed out.

In my view, midlife women will be the catalysts for creating positive change in our world. We have so much wisdom and experience to share. It has become the focus of my work to give women around the world the tools and strategies they are looking for to bring a spark back into their life.

What Will the Next 30 Years Look Like?

Have you ever taken an honest look at your plans for the next chapter in your life? If you are in your 50s or 60s, you need to be planning for at least another 30-40 years of contributing and sharing your gifts with the world. The old model of midlife and retirement told us we should plan to keep ourselves busy with gardening, travel, grandkids, and other fun things. These are all wonderful, but you might find yourself looking for something more stimulating after the first few months. These days 60 is the new 40! It's not the time to slow down. It's time to create the next chapter of your life.

I would venture a guess that most of us have an inner need to feel that we are contributing to our world in a valuable way. We need to know the reason why we get out of bed in the morning. The truth is, studies have shown that our 60s, 70s and 80s can be the most productive times in our lives! (SOURCE: New England Journal of Medicine 70,389, 2018)

Key Ingredients for Getting Out of Feeling Stuck and Alone

Stepping into the transformation that is part of a midlife awakening will bring about a wide range of challenges, adventures, and new opportunities. There are a few tips and tools that can help along the way. Here are a few of the lessons that I have learned.

- Take full responsibility for your own growth. Don't wallow in being a victim. Don't tolerate staying stuck.

- Allow yourself to take a deep, honest look at your own dreams and vision for your future. Creating clarity for yourself will give you the base to start building your next steps.

- Reflect on your inner beliefs and limitations. Are you feeling too old to start something new? Do you feel that no one values your wisdom and potential contributions? Allow yourself to challenge those beliefs and move past them. Open your eyes to the vast array of opportunities that are available to you. Ask yourself, What if .... What if these beliefs are not true? What if you're not too old and you're at the perfect age to start a new adventure? What if the world is waiting for you to share your wisdom and experience?

As you start your journey into this next chapter of your life, you may find that your immediate family and friends are not as supportive as you would like them to be. At times they might create major barriers to your progress. Keep in mind, they usually are simply trying to keep you safe and don't understand the changes you are trying to make. Hopefully, they will understand at some point, but in the meantime, create a community of supportive people around you. At this time in history, we have the advantage of technology that brings the whole world to you. Get adventuresome. Connect with new groups of people who inspire you to keep growing. Building a like-minded group of friends from around the world has been a wonderful experience for me.

Self-sabotaging thoughts and behaviours can keep us feeling stuck too. The best way to silence these voices is to take action toward your goals. Create your own evidence of success. Another valuable tool is observing other women taking action on the path you want to take. Seeing their success can reinforce your own strength to move forward. This is one of the things I love about books like this one. As women share their experiences, their challenges, and their triumphs with each other, we create a ripple effect of inspiration and leadership to help the readers take on life's adventures.

What is the legacy you want to leave in the world? Do you want your family and community to remember you as an inspiring role model, a woman of passion and integrity who created positive change in the world?

Creating these anthology books has become a major part of my work. Providing this platform for women to share their stories and inspire each other has become part of my legacy. These books will live on through generations. The women I have supported over the decades will create their own ripple effect of impact which will have far-reaching benefits to the world.

What is your WHY? What are those big dreams that you put on the back burner years ago? What is that new inspiration that has been nudging you forward?

This is one of my favourite quotes. It reminds me that taking on transformation in our lives will be uncomfortable and there will be challenges, but we need to stand firm in our decisions to follow our dreams.

How does one become a butterfly? You have to want to fly so much that you are willing to give up being a caterpillar.
~ Trina Paulus

Reignite your life! Allow yourself to dream. Give yourself permission to think of yourself and the life you want to create. Midlife women around the world are experiencing an awakening. Let's stand together and write the next chapter in history.

Cathy Derksen

Cathy Derksen is a catalyst and disruptor, supporting and inspiring midlife women to rediscover their brilliance and step into new possibilities. As the founder of her company Inspired Tenacity Global Solutions Inc, Cathy helps women take on the courage to face major changes in their lives. After working in finance for over a decade, she left her corporate job and started Inspired Tenacity to focus on helping women create success on their own terms.

Cathy is an international speaker and a 10x bestselling author who inspires her audience to dream big and take a leap of faith into reaching for their goals. She has created a platform supporting women to share their own inspiring stories in books, TV, and podcasts. With her all-in-one program, Cathy takes you from chapter concept to published bestselling author in a simple, exciting process.

Cathy lives near Vancouver, Canada. She has two children and 2 fur babies.

She enjoys spending time in nature, travelling, meeting new people, and connecting with her community around the world.

Connect with Cathy at https://inspiredtenacity.com.

CHAPTER 2

My Journey to Awakening

by Dr. Beatriz Olson MD, FACP

Would you not want to be the best version of yourself in this lifetime? After you die, would you not want to be remembered as someone who was authentic, deeply loved, and made a difference in the people around her? If the answer to these questions is yes, then you are either awakened or ready to be.

The definition of **awake** is being roused from sleep or to have a cause to stop sleeping. For the purposes of this spiritual sharing with you, sleep or sleeping means that you are living and accepting your life as your lot or karmic destiny. Perhaps you have not had the occasion to question if the life you are living and the beliefs that you have belong to you. Are your yearnings and dreams fulfilled? I have taken the time to ponder these and many more questions. I have gone through a journey of growth from disempowerment to empowerment and I hope my story inspires you to use the midlife transition as your launch pad to a fuller and healthier lifespan.

As a woman in her midlife, I understand what happens as we age and how we see ourselves. I am a Cuban woman who immigrated to America as a political refugee at the age of twelve. I worked really hard to succeed in all stages of my life; I wanted to make sure my parents knew that their sacrifice of leaving our country mattered. My father, a pediatrician, was punished for being anti-Castro after the early recognition that Castro would take away everyone's empowerment and freedom. After many years of emotional angst, my parents left Cuba. With four small children and no money, they were filled with hope and possibility. We lived for a year in Madrid, Spain, until our turn in the quota came, so we could enter America. This courageous and transformative choice that my parents made changed all of our lives.

When I came to America, I started to eat processed foods typical of the American diet. I went from a normal thin child to an obese teenager. There is a lot of bias against overweight and obese people and many people let me know that I had a problem. My cousins called me **fatso** and others called me **spic**. When you are a petite Cuban woman who is overweight, with an accent, and do not look like other people, it is not quite right. There are fewer jobs available at any age of our lives. I remember being told when I applied to be a server at the Scarsdale coffee shop that they could not consider me for a job because I was too short (at five feet) to reach the cash register. That day I walked home crying and my hard contact lenses scratched my corneas. I experienced severe pain and decreased vision. My body physically experienced the rejection I received in my heart's mind. Later on, I found there was limited compassion and perhaps prejudice from older people who strongly objected to my marriage to my husband. They said his marrying me would prevent him from becoming a society doctor.

I present my early experience for you to understand why all my life I aimed to be accepted, to please, and to try to belong. I share this because when you are an immigrant, you become *the other*. These early experiences affected me as a young person. Both my parents were medical professionals who worked all day. They could not be there to help me process the sense that something was seriously wrong with me, that I was not wanted or desired. These feelings early on disenfranchised me from my truth and myself. They took away my capacity to allow myself to be visible in my wholeness and created a sense of self-dissatisfaction. When others criticize you, sadly, it becomes part of you if you are young and not integrated. Early criticism not just hurts, but inevitably makes you become critical of yourself. You, therefore, may become perfectionistic in an effort to manage yourself and prevent further negative criticism from others. Perfectionism is the jail of a mind full of potential and limited possibility to express this potential.

I was fortunate to be born with an incredible amount of spirit energy which allowed me to have high drive and curiosity, despite the strange circumstances. I went on to get a great education and try to figure out the weight gain and appetite problem. Since then, I have had a stable weight, and have helped thousands of people do the same. I love living in my body. I honor it every day.

In medical school, I got very busy and found a place to belong. I learned that having been a dancer with the Cuban ballet as a child, and seeing the shaking hips of my relatives move to Cuban music, I could help assist with choreographing our medical school's Bard Hall Players. The yearly play happened to be *Pippin*, by Stephen Schwartz, a sumptuous space of intimacy and joy. That's how I got to know my future husband. He saw and heard who I was, and I saw and heard him. We began a conversation over champagne. Though coming from extremely different backgrounds, we were well met. We have had champagne for almost forty-two years and counting. Becoming a doctor at Columbia Medical School, developing the life-long friendships, discovering that there was goodness in me, that I could fall in love, that I help our community at the student and alumni level, was transformative to my well-being and self-esteem bank. I have been class chair, along with Eric, for the class of 1984.

A lot of water has run under the bridge in those four decades. I became an internist, then a basic and clinical scientist after my endocrinology fellowship and work at the National Institutes of Health. We waited many years after marriage, so we could be present for our children when they came. We had two daughters. They are now independent and successful women on their own. Being their mother humbled me from the time they were born. The love I felt when they were born taught me that, perhaps, my mother had loved me just as much when I came into the world. Being a mother tested me and at times brought me down to my knees, particularly as my daughters struggled to find their way back from illnesses or emotional setbacks. My societal mindsets and assumptions on motherhood helped and failed me. I tried my best at mothering: I was good enough, but never enough. When your mind has these beliefs and you have fixed ideas of what being a good mother is, there can be a lot of unnecessary suffering and questioning about the purpose and meaning of life.

I would like to add that being married for forty years is not easy. Especially when you have two independent, high-energy humans pursuing their professional lives and nurturing a family. I have learned that you can fall in and out of love multiple times, which reminds me, and perhaps it might you, about the song *Amie* by Pure Prairie League. The feeling that it is possible to fall back in love is inspiring, and doable. I have learned that making the effort to be friends, to have positive regard for each other, keeping emotional intimacy within, and seeing the newness that your partner is every day, may be the answer to long marriages that are healthy within. I think it is crucial to understand what your needs are at this midlife stage of your life, and that they are being met. If not, it is time to have a generative conversation, mutual growth orientation, with your partner. *How can we meet each other better?* If you cannot discuss or come to new terms of agreement, then you have choices: To accept and create with what is or to leave and create from without. Both ways can be rewarding if done wisely. Some of us women in more patriarchal and controlling societies may not have those choices. Then the only choice is to empower yourself to find joy in the space you are in.

I am an integrative endocrinologist, a medical doctor who uses western and eastern science and philosophy to help women with hormonal transitions of life. I have learned, personally used, and taught meditation as a method to connect the mind and body. When our body and mind are integrated, we can access our more advanced brain, our wisdom and spirit energy so we can create the environment and make choices to be healthy and thrive during transitions. The midlife menopausal transition is a complex time. You may remember that when you went through puberty, when you had the hormone swings and mood changes of your monthly lunar menstrual cycles, and after you gave birth that it caused shifts in you that, regardless of age, made you pay attention to your body and state of being.

Menopause is another of those times. Our hormones go and often no one helps to replace them. When hormones are replaced, we can regain our hormone balance. The loss of our hormones, like estrogen and progesterone, causes havoc. We are programmed at this time to stop contributing to the universe. Since we are beyond the stage of fulfilling our task to reproduce and help the next generation survive, there was no evolutionary pressure for women to maintain their healthy levels of hormones.

With the loss of estrogen, progesterone, and testosterone, we begin to age faster. It is unfair, but ancestral pressures over millennia created this pattern for women. In the past, we died early. In our modern world we live longer but may not have a healthy lifespan. I do not believe we should accept this ancestral destiny physically, or its effects on our minds, biology and potential. I am a proponent of keeping healthy hormone levels as we age, by replacing our hormones wisely, if we do not have genetic risks for breast cancer. Even if we did not get hormone replacement, our brains and nerve cells do continue to work at this time. I found it rewarding during my transition to actively focus on creating and making new connections in my brain by engaging and learning new things. We can give ourselves the gift of trying new things - just for fun and without judgment.

Midlife is a time when life outside of us is also changing. Our children have gone to university and colleges and are finding their own lives. This is a time of transitions for our intimate relations. It is good to spend time reassessing and perhaps redefining our focus and connection to children and partners. This is an opportunity to awaken and question everything thoughtfully and compassionately. When we are in this period of our lives, we have gathered so much experience, resilience and grit. We have serious wisdom and developed a full and soulful heart. When we embrace and connect to these inner powers that we own, we catapult ourselves to a new level of being. A level where we let go of the façades we have used to hide ourselves. We let go of trying so hard, which is depleting, when we in fact have done more than enough. It's a time to shed old mindsets and fear-based behaviors that limit our potential about who we are, and what we can and cannot do. When we wake up and embrace our wholeness we recognize that our worth was never negotiable. We were born into this world where we inherently belong. Know that we are now the wise women. We have unique gifts to give to the world with our presence. Let's get up from our sleep and awaken. Awaken to our truth, potential and new horizons.

Dr. Beatriz Olson

Dr. Beatriz Olson is a unique transformational leader. She is an integrative endocrinologist who offers a comprehensive and multidisciplinary approach to healing. She has decades of experience and deep expertise in caring for women and their hormones. She combines evidence-based science, mind-body and functional medicine to help her clients. She has transformed thousands of patients' health for the better. As a woman physician and Cuban immigrant, she has learned to overcome many life challenges. She teaches awareness and skills to overcome that which limits potential and makes us sick.

Dr. Olson is board-certified in the fields of Endocrinology, Metabolism and Diabetes, and Internal Medicine. She has certifications in Age Management Medicine and Feminine Power Transformational Leadership. She graduated from Barnard College, Columbia University College of Physicians and Surgeons; both her internship and residency in internal medicine and research-clinical fellowship in Endocrinology were at the University of Pittsburgh. She served as clinical faculty and scientist at the National Institutes of Health, and is past clinical faculty at

Yale University School of Medicine. She has authored numerous basic science and clinical articles in peer-reviewed journals and contributed chapters to several textbooks. She resides with her husband Dr. Eric J Olson in Connecticut, USA.

Connect with Beatriz at www.beatrizolson.com.

Photo credit: Kris Kinsley Hancock

CHAPTER 3

Midlife Awakening Under an African Mango Tree

by Beth Harkins

There seems to not be an agreed upon definition of midlife in today's world. Is it age thirty, forty, fifty or could it be sixty? What is an awakening anyway? Is there a single awakening that can shift the rest of our lives? On the day of my unexpected, powerful midlife awakening, I did not know the answers to any of these questions, nor had it occurred to me to ask them.

Something happened merely weeks before I turned forty-nine. On a Monday morning, after arriving at my school office, I hurried to my desk to complete my monthly parent newsletter. Before rereading it, I paused to consider the past eleven years working as the school's curriculum coordinator and parent educator. Many challenges and many rewards had come my way through relationships with young people, parents and colleagues.

While previous extensive world travel had taken a backseat, I had delighted in watching our daughter's growth and development at the school. The supportive and encouraging learning environment was beneficial to so many of the young people in attendance. Because of my history with my job, I struggled to make sense of a sudden and dramatic workplace culture shift. One day the head of our school shockingly declared that our environment was growing too soft and feminized. He said he wanted to beef up and clean up the curriculum. His comments seemed unimaginable coming from a man I thought I knew well. He also shared that he wanted student reading lists reviewed without specifying a review committee.

I realized that diversity and inclusion, with respect for the rights of women and girls, would no longer be a recognized operating principle. I feared that the parenting advice I had been welcome to share in the past, would be replaced by a punitive, shame-filled, authoritarian approach. That same approach would affect the way teachers were expected to handle their classrooms.

The worst part was that I could not muster the courage to raise concerns to my male boss. Fear of the intimidating power of male authority left me believing my words would get stuck in my throat. I felt certain that trying to speak, while filled with anger and irritation, I would flush with emotion and might be unable to breathe. I was in agony, looking for a way to deal with despair I did not know how to manage. I put the newsletter aside and rushed to write a resignation letter. I felt like a complete failure reacting in such an unassertive manner.

The painful resignation proved to be nothing more than a silent retreat from the unacceptable. Post resignation, lost in depression and self-blame, I had no idea where I would find another job. Complicating matters further, the loss of my income challenged my husband and I to provide the education we wanted to give our daughter as she headed to college. Rudderless, empty, and scared, I did not know who I was anymore. Despite an intense passion to connect with the rise of the feminine, I could not see a path to play my part.

While confused and blaming myself for a lack of courage, I recalled a time when I lived in Casablanca, Morocco. It was 1953, I was a precocious, green-eyed, freckled faced, six-year-old, American girl with bangs, and plenty of attitude. While enjoying life in Morocco, where my father, an Air Force Lieutenant Colonel, was stationed, I listened to my mother tell stories about the newly crowned Queen Elizabeth. About Athena, the Greek goddess of wisdom and power and about powerful Queen Cleopatra and the much-loved Goddess Isis.

Running around the banana tree in the front yard of our white stucco home, I imagined myself as a powerful queen or goddess. Inhaling the scent of purple bougainvillea near our house, I believed all horizons were open to me.

I decided I wanted earrings like those worn by queens and goddesses. My older Arab playmate understood because she had earrings. Since Mother said I was too young for earrings, Votna stepped in with her a string, needle and tiny beads prepared to make me earrings and to pierce my ears. I felt no pain, as her needle entered first one, then the other earlobe. Only delight did I feel when I touched tiny beads dangling from the string.

When Mother saw the dirty strings, she swiftly cut them. With that action, my magical power disappeared. Forlorn, I waited for my tall, strong father to come home. I wanted to sit on his lap and hear him say I was beautiful, wonderful, and smart, despite not having earrings. Instead, he arrived home and told me to sit still, be quiet and don't interrupt.

As I sat silencing myself on the floor outside the living room, my father and his Air Force officer friends discussed world affairs. I concluded my father's world was reserved for men and my world would be one of invisibility and inferiority. I no longer believed I could become a queen or a goddess in a world with all horizons open to me.

What was I to do? Who would I become? I shrunk down inside the limiting story I told myself. The years rolled past like unnoticed clouds. Unnoticed, like me.

The years rolled on. After college graduation, I heard that Pan American World Airways was interviewing for stewardesses to fly on the new jumbo jets that were carrying jetsetters around the world. Because I spoke Spanish, and could meet the required height and weight limits, I was hired. I moved from my home in Oklahoma City and settled in Miami, Florida. After training, I took off to see the world wearing a blue uniform, felt bolo hat, gloves, regulation make-up and hairdo, plus pantyhose and heels. When not traveling, I got a master's in humanistic psychology and led women's consciousness raising groups. I was certain that women held the key to bringing balance to an out of balance world. All the while, I carried baggage. A hidden story of self-doubt and not enough-ness.

During my worldwide quest to find my voice and value, I met the amazing man who became my husband. He allowed me to face many doubts, though I could not wash them all away. In time, we became parents to a precious daughter. I left Pan Am when we moved across the country. My deep desire was to assure our daughter would claim her voice and know how to take her place in the world. I watched with delight as she grew to do exactly that. When I felt attempts to suppress the feminine voice at my workplace, my abrupt resignation followed as did my deep despair.

One evening as I soaked in the bathtub, for a brief moment, I considered putting my head under the water to end my feelings of worthlessness. The next thing I knew, my husband arrived holding the phone and announcing I had a call waiting. I wrapped myself in a towel as I took the phone. I heard a voice ask if I would interview for a travel coordinator position with an international non-governmental organization. Prior to forwarding a resume in response to a notice about the position, I never imagined such work existed.

A week later I was hired to lead groups of financial supporters to villages in remote areas of Asia, Africa, and Latin America. We would visit grassroots programs led by local leaders trained to improve food security, health, education, and the creation of small businesses. What excited me most was the chance to see how the lives of impoverished women, living in situations beyond my imagination, were finding hope and possibility through the trainings. What I could not have imagined was the hope and possibility I would find for my own life. Below is the story that made my new mid-life story unfold.

It was a hot, steamy day in a remote farming village in Western Kenya. I sat under the splayed branches of a wild mango tree surrounded by brown millet stalks, mud huts and a circle of village women wrapped in multi-colored, bold patterned, cotton fabric known as kanga cloth.

The mango tree shade had a history as space for men only. One of few trees in the village, it had been off limits to women who were told poisonous snakes rested in the shade of the tree. It was believed the women would be bitten by the snakes, while the men somehow could protect themselves. But things were changing.

The women had learned that when planting, they could space their corn seeds in rows rather than broadcasting them as in the past. Using fewer corn seeds and less water they could produce more corn to feed their families, with corn left to sell at the market. With the money earned, they created a savings and micro-credit program that allowed one woman at a time to purchase a cow.

Because of growing successes, for the first time, the women were seen to have worth. They had the power to negotiate with the men for time to sit and enjoy the shade. On the day of our arrival, we greeted a circle of women with snake sticks nearby. They held not fear, but rather anticipation for more changes they could create.

For the members of Wasiwasi Women's Circle, the snake had become a feminine symbol. They understood that as snakes must shed their old skin, so must women shed their old stories of invisibility and unworthiness.

After serving tea boiled over an open fire, one by one the women rose to speak. "Mercy Akoth, president, *Wasiwasi* Women's Group," the first woman proudly announced. We discovered *wasiwasi* means sweat in Swahili. The kind that forms on the women's brows as they labor in the fields and labor delivering and caring for children and labor through new endeavors. Together we clapped and supported each woman's sharing.

The moment arrived for the last woman to stand and speak. Drawing a slow, deep breath, the woman paused. The group waited in full support. I wondered if we would hear this shy, reserved woman speak.

I watched and saw this woman straighten her spine, raise her chin and take a deep breath. Then I heard these words, "Cecilia Adhiambo, a new memba of Wasiwasi." Her syllables resonated like an African drumbeat echoing the power and possibility of long-silenced women.

Every cell in my body expanded. Rather than feeling my body constrict, I felt filled with feminine power. I knew I would dedicate my life to support women like Cecelia in bringing forward their voices and the transformational forces women hold inside each of our stories.

The energy of Wasiwasi Women's Circle that supported Cecelia's rise to speak, simultaneously awakened my lost voice. I felt something shift. The victim in me disappeared and my heroine's journey began.

Soon I began to lead groups of American women across Asia, Africa, and Latin America to visit other inspiring women's groups. Together we witnessed women harvesting innovative ideas and creating new resources, even in the face of seemingly insurmountable obstacles.

Such is the pathway to confidence and courage I experienced thanks to a midlife awakening under a mango tree in a rural African village. I realize awakening and empowerment do not happen in one moment. The journey often takes time with dips and dives. As women we each need support from others. We require encouragement to try new things. To work to release old patterns of invisibility, of not enoughness, of holding back, of feeling unsafe, and of limiting ourselves. When we learn how we have blocked ourselves, we can speak up and awaken to new possibilities. Finally, it becomes possible to acknowledge that staying silent, or invisible without self-care and self-love does not suit us anymore. We realize the world needs our wisdom and innate knowing and sharing this feels good at any age.

Beth Harkins

Beth Harkins is an inspiring speaker, a trained transformational women's coach and facilitator, as well as the author of the highly acclaimed novel, The Possibility of Everywhere: Casablanca to Oklahoma City, Kathmandu to Timbuktu. She has gathered women's stories across sixty-five countries on six continents. At one time she spent six months crossing the backroads of the USA to hear what mid-life women had to say about their lives.

Beth's education and professional training have given her skills and insights for both writing and working with women. Yet what most informs her work has come from listening to hundreds of women's stories. Whether successful c-suite executive women in high-rise office buildings or poverty-stricken rural village women who fetch and carry water on their heads, Beth has discovered how much the desire and the struggle to be seen, heard, and valued impacts women's lives.

Beth believes women cannot become themselves by themselves, that women's stories matter and that how women tell their stories to themselves and others shapes their lives and can shape the world.

Connect with Beth at https://linktr.ee/bethharkins.

CHAPTER 4

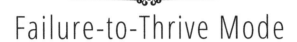

Failure-to-Thrive Mode

by Beth Jaffe

The 2020 global pandemic brought a lot of people to their knees where they began to discover their humble meek natures. People on their knees are praying or seeking mercy or relief from suffering. It's a very human thing to do, and often the discovery of one's humble meek nature leads one to also find true magical joy. I was no stranger to suffering and magical joy so when the dark cloud of 2020 rolled in, I knew that eventually there'd be one heck of a rainbow showing up. I believe rainbows are like human souls and trees falling in the forest. They exist, with or without witnesses, in their full glory; sounds, colors, and all.

Let's look at the first seeds of my Midlife Awakening. I was four or five, having breakfast with my grandparents. My grandmother was snapping orders about manners. I dropped my spoon into my cereal and looked her straight in the eyes. I said, "Grandma, you give me a headache." My grandpa laughed himself silly. I had stunned us all and briefly enjoyed the relief that came from claiming my right to slouch and relish Grandpa's laughter. Grandma tried scolding both of us, but Grandpa's laughter gave her permission to lighten up. He had the best laugh.

Moving along the timeline of my life, these bright-light kind of moments thin out. What we really need to remember is that in my world, girls did not have the freedom boys did. We girls had to face an overwhelming standard of strict expectations, while the boys were encouraged to explore their many freedoms. Girls were trained to tolerate a lowly status in the home, as well as the outside world. Cultural norms held us bound to confusing unspoken rules. We learned to be very hard on ourselves for survival.

Wanting our home life to be a safe haven, my sister and I often complained of the double standard we saw, but to no avail. I cried to my father, "But it's not fair!"

His voice thundered with a fierce rage that I can still feel, "who told you life would be fair? Life is not fair and don't you forget it!" Forty years later, just thinking of that voice makes me want to run for my life. Since I don't care for running, I easily slip into the other standard responses; fight, freeze, or people please. Gladly, I can say because of my Midlife Awakening and focusing on my soul's joy, my ability to respond to old triggers in new ways is gaining positive momentum. I've stopped pathologizing my survival mechanisms so I'm responding better than ever before.

Looking back, it's maddening to remember the mixed messages. Right next to expecting me to accept injustice, my father was also very clear with that scary voice, "No daughter of mine will be a nurse! You'll be a doctor or the head of the hospital. Get used to that now." Obviously, I avoided healthcare related careers, because that voice and those words together sent fear into the depths of my bones.

Facing the daily onslaught of all that senseless "because I said so" from the people in power positions, I created a vast network of thought patterns based entirely on avoiding the pain and confusion born from feeling so powerless all the time. Thoughts oriented on avoidance fail to focus on positive possibilities. My thoughts geared so intensely toward avoiding all the negative stuff became chains that held me bound to an invisible jail. I had no idea I was spending my life building a mental cage of tragically misguided decisions based on false assumptions.

During early adulthood, due to circumstances beyond my control, these unconscious and ruthless thought patterns took charge of my mind and basically ruled the days of my adult life. I was like a tiger on a golden-chained leash, until one of my sons graduated from high school. On that day, a part of me found the weak link. I wasn't strong enough to break it but sitting in that big building full of all those people beaming with pride at the sea of youth walking their rite of passage, I felt it. Something important shifted.

My mom was sitting next to me. She felt it too. She looked at me with big loving eyes and said, "I'm so proud of you." I didn't burst into tears, but wanted to. It would have been such a wonderful release. However, old habits have their place too. Thanks to all that training to hide emotions which some, like my mother, still consider weaknesses, I managed to keep my composure and smile with a few socially acceptable token tears. I was in my mid-forties at the time, and I could have felt proud of myself for plenty of both soft and solid reasons. Sadly, instead of pride, confidence, and self-assuredness I felt a huge sticky hole inside.

I want to dive deep into the proof of my success and wellness while illustrating the objectively impressive and positive aspects of my life prior to this high school graduation moment. I also feel the need to describe the negative mental chains and the way they held my inner prison intact. These things next to each other would give you an image worth pondering. However, as a comfortable white woman with an elite level bachelor's degree and tons of bold life experience far beyond the average range, I should not be complaining of any hints of displeasure or hardship.

I've known all along, even while eating cereal at Grandma's, that I'm living an amazing life. I've seen others marvel at me as I felt myself blundering through the years. I've always been fully capable and even obligated to step into big leadership roles. From the outside I've mostly appeared to be a trailblazing female of substance. The truth is: the feelings I imagined I'd feel if I were all that have been painfully elusive. I haven't felt free or powerful. I haven't felt the flow of positive growth cycles and comfortable living. I've felt scared, lost, deeply frustrated, and taken for granted. I've felt like a doormat for people and worse, for the people I love. I've felt frozen in time and unable to excel in ways that make sense to me. I've felt desperately trapped, lonely, and hopeless that my life would be anything other than an example of what not to be.

My success in life has been connected to a series of in-spite-of stories. Of all I know about what not to do and who not to be, the most important take home message is this: never become a birthmother. Birthmothers are women who face an unplanned pregnancy and relinquish their parental rights, sometimes even before giving birth. Don't do this, don't let people you love do this, and don't even let your worst enemy do this. I say this because I've lived with this decision for over thirty years, and I've been an activist in this arena. I changed a law related to adoption. I've known enough birthparents and adults who have been adopted to say with confidence: the soul crushing anguish and grief, along with the mental chains that develop directly due to the choice of adoption are extremely bad. In my case, the experience was a deep and abiding trauma that led to a mental health crisis just before my twenty-first birthday, plenty of subsequent years spent dancing on the edges of a mental health crisis, and decades of living stuck in a failure-to-thrive mode. Those who lose their children to adoption are silently suffering in ways society refuses to acknowledge. Therapists trained in birthmother trauma are rarer than birthmother support groups. No acknowledgment of the problem means no solutions. The birthmother's experience is very grim.

Let's let this sink in. From shortly after my high school graduation until my late forties, I lived with hidden trauma, unresolvable grief, a general sense of not thriving, and frankly no hope of ever being truly happy again. Even with professional help, a dreamy husband, good career options, a lovely home, and three fun sons I was able to raise pretty darn well, I suffered unnecessarily. Tolerating mental chains and unfair societal rules lead to the adoption and so many challenges afterward. I wrote a memoir about this big slice of my life because my Midlife Awakening is helping me heal the trauma.

During those hectic years of raising my other three sons, my mental health was fine enough. I had been through enough therapy and lived enough to know that I was responding to the days of my life well enough. But I developed serious physical health issues. Looking back, I can now see these were in part psychosomatic. At the time, I couldn't see that because I was so functional. I found traditional medicine unsatisfactory in helping me find my health, hope and joy. In spite of meeting my son lost to adoption, deep resources, and amazing capacities, I could not get well nor could I improve my ability to enjoy life, until I almost died of covid. My covid-related near-death experience was in fact, the blooming of my Midlife Awakening. Ever since, I have been better than ever because I know what a gift life is.

Back at my son's graduation, that shift, that sticky hole, and those few tears that dripped down while I watched all those young people walking into their future... it all added up to an awareness which pushed its tender shoots out of the soil of my silent suffering and into the light of my life. I was filled with hope that perhaps I could rediscover my youthful sense of boundless and expansive joy. I began noticing my tolerations for all the unspoken rules I was following. I started wondering what would happen if I developed an intolerance for being so tolerant.

I vowed to find inner soul-based happiness instead of wearing my mask of pretend happy. I said yes to a friend who wanted me to join her on a cruise, because I always wanted to go on a cruise and my husband didn't. I committed to daily meditation with an App that kept track for me. I took a break from helping everyone else all the time. I mothered myself in new and improved ways. My steps were slow and unsteady during those first years of truly awakening because those delicate tender shoots of joy meant big changes too. Even good change can be scary.

Waking up can require a few hits on the snooze button, especially if awakening means wading through trauma and unresolvable grief. Egos are such important survivalist personalities living inside us. Any inner adventure requires making friends with one's ego and eventually helping the ego to let go of control. Egos don't like change. They like control and the metaphoric snooze button.

Raising sons and working in a male-dominated office, I didn't have to face some of my ego's subtle tricks. When I first started truly growing my own happiness, I began surrounding myself with more women. This led to noticing my ego's mysterious ways. It wasn't always comfortable work, but I persistently dropped that which I tolerated in order to pick up new experiences and new friendships. I quit my job without a real plan for bringing in income. My husband stumbled with me on that one. But like I said, he's dreamy and we recovered. He agreed to finally take the kids to Europe because he realized I was going with or without him. It was 2019.

In 2020 when I woke up from my near-death experience, I stopped waiting for my lost son, the alarm clock, or even rainbows. I went deeper with my commitment to love myself and wondered how to become the answer to my prayers. I'm beyond 2200 consecutive days of meditation now. My humble steps are strong and steady. I'm in love with life itself.

And I'm just getting started. The end/beginning.

Beth Jaffe

Beth Jaffe is first and foremost an erudite mystic. Her free spirit precedes her and people who meet her speak of her gentle nature, joyful sense of wonder, and surprising mix of other qualities. Artist and activist by nature; entrepreneur by design, Beth loves the creative process. By dedicating herself to finding ways to express the unspoken, she works to spread joy, strengthen hope, and nourish the beautiful dreams of an evolving world perfecting itself.

Beth's love for the natural world bloomed at age ten when she fell in love with Montana on her way to Yellowstone Park during a family trip. While studying Natural Resources at Cornell University in the late '80s and early '90s, Beth developed her own independent study program in computer graphics and animation. Though she once vowed to never use computers again and didn't for several years, she helped her husband raise a software company while raising three sons. They are especially proud of PantrySoft which helps food pantries across the globe feed people facing food insecurity. In 2015, Beth changed a Montana state law related to adoption because of her experience with an unplanned pregnancy.

Beth's budding writing career is rooted in her curiosity about dyslexia, creativity, and mental health. In addition to writing, she is currently offering one on one coaching sessions and group workshops for those longing to develop their creativity and to transform their life from a dreadful slog into an extraordinary adventure.

Connect with Beth at https://www.bethjaffe.com.

CHAPTER 5

Livestreaming Saved Me from Myself

by Bridgetti Lim Banda

I recall the ache from deep within me to have children and to be the best version of a mom I could possibly be. I was in my late twenties when we got married, and I had very fixed ideas of what I wanted, but nothing prepares one for the many challenges that come with raising a family. Getting pregnant wasn't that difficult, although it took a good couple of months, but I quickly discovered it was not that easy maintaining my pregnancies, thanks to endometriosis and chronic back and neck pain. Raising children can be a challenging yet very rewarding experience. It takes a lot of hard work, patience, and dedication to successfully guide children through the various phases of life.

During this time, parents need to work together as a team to ensure their children's physical, emotional, and psychological well-being. It can have a profound impact on a marriage. If parents don't work to meet the needs of their children, their relationship with each other may become strained. It leads to feelings of resentment, guilt, and frustration. Navigating the complexities of parenting can put a strain on even a healthy marriage. Having to deal with several health challenges led to lots of moments of conflict and resentment and the growing frustration of not being fully in control of my body. Well-meaning friends and family didn't help. I was on a long journey of self-discovery.

It wasn't until much later in my life that I discovered the complexities of my invisible diseases and how it led me to make choices I may otherwise not have made. Desperation for pain relief very nearly cost me my life. What was meant to be a brief stay in hospital for a routine hysterectomy turned into a nightmare with seven days in ICU, three of which I was unconscious, and a further twenty-one-day stay in the hospital ward before being released for recovery at home.

This episode plunged me into early menopause, and reactions from friends and family were varied and confusing. What I learnt from the experience is that you cannot satisfy everyone in your life, and sometimes you simply need to push others' feelings aside and do what feels right for you. Given my health challenges, much as I would have loved to have another baby, it would have put my life at risk.

The teenage years were eventful and rewarding, and as my sons grew older, I started realising there was a gap in my life and I could slowly start filling my cup with things I enjoy and that make me happy. I've always enjoyed giving of myself to others, and spending hours talking to friends and family as they neared the end of their lives was something that filled my cup. Each experience was different and unique, and I enjoyed the gift of bringing joy and relief to others from their pain. If anything, it was a great way of deflecting from my own pain. I knew if I could keep my mind occupied, it would prevent me from falling into depression and feeling sorry for myself.

This worked for a really long time, until my body became so worn down with pain that I could no longer ignore it, and again I was confronted with making surgical choices that could have a huge impact on my future. Given the fact that my pain became debilitating to the point I was starting to feel life was no longer worth living, I took the plunge and had the surgery. Recovery was a long process. It gave me back renewed zeal to carry on with my purpose for serving others. Just a few years later, I was again confronted with making another surgical choice I didn't want to make. I needed neck surgery, and it scared me to death. The prospect of a failed procedure was scary, but I had no choice. The pain was too intense to ignore. I'm not sure when things shifted, but I suddenly realised I'd reached a point where others' opinions didn't matter so much and I could start making guilt-free choices. I decided to have the surgery and was ready to deal with whatever life handed me after that. My sons were young adults, and I knew that whatever happened, they would be okay.

Whilst I was waiting for surgery, I was filled with many mixed emotions, but one thing was certain: my choices came from a different place. A place of knowing what I wanted, perhaps even selfishly so. I was determined to have a better quality of life and discovered there were other avenues I could pursue that would still fill my cup even when my body let me down. I wanted a more meaningful life, something I could carve around my challenges of living with chronic pain. First, I had to accept that chronic pain was part of who I had become but that I did not want to be defined by it. I had to find ways from deep within my soul to accept what I could not change and to embrace what I could do to fill my cup. A huge part of this transformation process was gratitude. Learning to focus on what I could do and not so much what I no longer could do.

It was at this point in my life that Periscope emerged—a livestreaming tool, one of many other such tools and technologies to follow—and I finally discovered something that filled my cup. Learning to put myself out in the public domain was overwhelming and scary, but my desire to serve my community and to be able to do something I could do from a home studio and work around my chronic pain was larger. It opened up a floodgate of opportunities I could never have imagined.

It was at this point that I reflected on how my role in the family had changed too. My children were carving their own lives and were no longer so dependent on me. I remember rushing through my lunch one day and then stopped and smiled, when I realised I no longer needed to rush through my meals to tend to a child. I could actually sit down, relax, and enjoy my food, *and* cook what I enjoyed.

Through the childrearing years, friendships were mostly decided on by whomever my children were attracted to, and restaurant outings were limited to family friendly establishments. It was as if a whole new world had suddenly emerged. Although I appreciated the friendships formed by the choices my children made, I realised I now had the opportunity to start rekindling friendships I had before I started my family and make new ones. Friendships of my own making. It also dawned on me that I could start choosing to support more refined dining experiences. How did this happen? The unfolding process of this new life was gradual, liberating, and exciting, spoiled only by the intensity of my chronic pain episodes.

Midlife is an exciting time realising you have the opportunity to explore new opportunities that were not possible whilst raising a family. The world suddenly becomes your oyster. You can learn a new language, take up a new hobby, go to new places for vacations, volunteer, and even explore, do more that fills your spiritual cup, and of course, for me, remain within the limits of what my physical body could tolerate. I could either allow myself to sink into depression about what my body could no longer do, or I could embrace what I could do. I chose the latter.

Even though I was dumped into a chemical menopause at an early age, the effects have lived on much longer than expected. A roller coaster ride no woman wants to stay on, and I have wished so many times that the ride would come to an end. Even on the edge of fifty-eight years of age, I still live with the effects of menopause. A friend affectionately dubbed it tropical moments. Truth be told, I'd much rather actually be on a tropical island, sipping copious amounts of margaritas and mojitos in the cool breeze of the ocean, than trying to swim my way through dripping perspiration episodes that leave me feeling as if I am drowning in my own sweat. Oh, the joys of menopause, and I wish someone would just hit the damn pause button so I could get on with life!

Getting back to wanting to focus on serving others and not allowing myself to have too much time to spend on feeling sorry for myself and what I could no longer do, I started my journey of discovery to find out what I could focus on as a topic for livestreaming. Initially, I felt I wanted to delve into creating more awareness around invisible disabilities, but the topic was way too close to home. I didn't think I had the mental and emotional strength it took to remain focused whilst my body was riddled with pain.

Thankfully, for me, the Cape Town water crisis was beginning to emerge, and I realised that was the opportunity of a lifetime. Water was being weaponised, and ordinary people wanted facts and information that was not politicised and which they could use to make informed choices and decisions vital for survival. I knew nothing about water other than being a user along with my fellow citizens, but I realised that if I could learn to livestream and convince water professionals to be interviewed, I could fill a valuable role. So armed only with an intense desire to make a difference, I failed my way forward through livestreaming, and to my surprise, the water professionals said yes! Very quickly, I had a huge social media following with people eager for their voices to be heard and hanging on for information. Before long, I had an established live TV show with a large following.

To my surprise, I was suddenly inundated with requests for interviews from mainstream television and radio stations from around the globe. Because Cape Town is such a huge tourist attraction, there was much interest in what was happening on the ground, and media houses wanted in on the local stories. Journalists contacted me for news articles, and it was just the craziest time of my life. This was a huge learning curve and my baptism into the world of livestreaming.

The next crisis was the Covid pandemic, and that too allowed me to share the concerns of my community. Shared experiences brought comfort at a time when people felt alone and isolated due to lockdowns and misinformation. Mental health was at an all-time low, with people losing their livelihoods, and having an outlet to talk was hugely helpful.

Fast forward a couple of years, I have also been producing and hosting an author show for almost five years running. In fact, I now produce and host two author shows. In addition, I became the first person in Africa to get access to LinkedIn Live, a global livestreaming platform that caters strictly to the business community. A privilege indeed! The cherry on the cake was also becoming the first Amazon Live Influencer in Africa, to the best of my knowledge. I can truly and honestly say livestreaming has saved me from myself. It has opened doors and opportunities I never thought were possible. It allows me to work around my chronic pain from my home studio, and I am truly thankful for the opportunities to serve others and that it does not leave me with time to sink into depression, because the journey of living with invisible illnesses where people around you constantly try to invalidate and minimise and even speak dismissively of your pain is a life filled with many challenges and frustrations. People don't easily sympathise with an affliction they cannot visibly see. Now that I am in a much more empowered space, speaking out more about invisible disabilities is definitely on my bucket list.

Bridgetti Lim Banda

Bridgetti Lim Banda is a Digital Storytelling Advocate who helps entrepreneurs, authors, thought leaders, and businesses share their stories to increase brand awareness and engagement.

Connect with Bridgetti at www.blivemedia.com.

In Alignment with My Purpose

by Ewa Krempa

"Let us not look back in anger nor forward in fear but around us in awareness." – Leland Val Van De Wall

---

In my younger years, I filled my life with adventures, but there was always something stopping me from fully enjoying my life.

In spring of 2000, I went on a High School Europe trip to five countries: Germany, The Netherlands, France, Belgium and Luxembourg, where my passion for travel grew even stronger. I eagerly graduated high school and went straight into the Travel and Tourism Industry. When Travel and Tourism was not up to the full speed I was looking for, I found myself exploring other job avenues. Overall, they did not satisfy my true passion in life.

A few years later, I went on a humanitarian trip to El Salvador with World Vision Canada. We built a home for a family, visited a few of the local communities there and connected with many kids as we cooked and played with them. Giving them gifts, showing them how to play and watching them laugh and play with joy was a priceless experience. It was a revelation on so many levels for me. I knew in my heart I had a calling to help people, and that some day I could do much more. With my love for adventure, when the project ended, I continued a solo journey across to Honduras, Nicaragua, Costa Rica and to Panama before returning home to Canada. I was a bit nervous doing this portion of the trip on my own, but the universe had my back. It was truly the most rewarding experience I have had up to that point in my life.

It was in 2006 that I was introduced to the movie *The Secret* by Rhonda Byrne and began to understand the Law of Attraction. Prior to her movie and books, I hadn't given thought to the Law of Attraction or even knew what it was all about.

I used some of that knowledge to attract more travelling into my life. For years, I was looking at pictures of the amazing places around the world and when the opportunity knocked on the door in September 2010 to circumnavigate around the world, I took it in a heartbeat. There are some events in life that define you forever. It can be a moment, a trip, or meeting someone for the first time. Nothing on earth had shaped me more, at that time, than the eight months I spent sailing around the world.

Continuing my travel throughout the last two and a half decades has led me to so many experiences. Amongst some of my favorites were swimming with the dolphins, ziplining, sky diving, visiting NASA and the Atlantis Hotel in Dubai, as well as eating at 7-Star restaurants, and riding a camel at Petra like Indiana Jones in the movies. It goes without saying that meeting many wonderful people around the world including Queen Elizabeth II was truly amazing. It's those in-between moments that truly shape who you are.

All this sounds amazing, right? Well, it sure was, and I would have had it all, were it not for events of my childhood and the choices of my young adulthood. They affected me in ways that lead me to simply not know how to cope with looking thru a pieced together perception of a child's mind.

As a young child, I found out that my biological mom had passed away due to cancer within six months of my birth, and my biological father was not able to take care of me. I was put into a foster home until age three, when another family adopted me. All these early years were in southern Poland, until 1993, when my parents decided to move to Canada. New country, big city, not a word of English, no friends & missing family back home had left me emotionally broken.

In 2000, when I was eighteen, I took an Autumn trip to Europe. It was then that I was first introduced to my biological family. I learned that I had siblings and cousins and grandparents who had stayed together in Poland, after I had been adopted and moved across the world. In my head, I was trying to piece together fragments of my world as I was living in it and why my life was the way it was. Why did I have to go thru so many experiences, while all the other kids had normal lives? At school, I was not comfortable in my own skin, I disliked presentations. I did not have many friends, except the ones I had, I held close to my heart. As an eager teen, I had many interests; I was very successful in the All-City orchestra, karate lessons and winning art awards. Still, I couldn't wait to be done with high school.

The lack of awareness of my true relationship with the infinite power, for many years, left me with a distorted image of myself. I felt invisible. For years to come, my thoughts were fueled by ghosts of anger, fear, lack of confidence and no self-love, playing on autopilot in the back of my mind.

I can say that I entertained the opposing and contradictory ideas for far too long. Over the years, a lot of my mental activity had led me to stress, exhaustion and failing health. What was worse was that at the time I thought I could not do anything about it. I had felt part of my identity fading away.

When I look back, all along, the two things that gave me solace were traveling and believing in a power greater than myself, believing in God. Travelling was like escaping from the present reality and believing in God gave me hope for a better tomorrow.

A new perception of reality – my awakening

In 2018, my daughter came into my life. Soon after, in 2021, I came to realize that staying where I was, in my current mindset, was no longer an option. I did not have a bad life. In fact, things were rather good, but I knew I could do so much more with my life, if only I could have believed and had faith in myself and my abilities. The minute I made that decision, doors opened for me.

"When the student is ready the teacher will appear."
~Tao Te Ching

With that, Bob Proctor teachings have come back into my life, and for the first time I took these teachings about the Law of Attraction to the next level. Bob helped me identify what I'd never considered, that which set me up to practice and integrate new ways of thinking into my daily routines. I needed to reshape my life; the stories of my past were the same, but I began to give them a new meaning.

What I learned was that whenever we wish to receive anything new in our life, we must trigger the process by making room for it. I started to consider what I needed to let go of that no longer served me, what

I wanted to hold on to that was meaningful, and what I wanted and needed to learn anew.

I learned that this law applied to not only to my physical world, but also to my metal domain. To clarify, that whenever we wish to entertain new ideas, we must first be willing to let go of, or to challenge some of our old ones. For me there were a lot of them. I began playing with my imagination and thought about what kind of future I wanted and what mindset and new paradigms would best contribute to that future. I started to pay attention, imagine possibilities, and intentionally practice new ways of thinking and acting what I felt were in alignment with the new future I wanted to manifest and experience.

These new practices, from numerous programs, began to replace and modify the mindset that was, and new possibilities began to appear. The new outlook I adapted for life required discipline, and I will not lie that there were good days and days that I greatly struggled. My life began to expand and grow in new directions. A whole new world was shaping in my imagination and mirroring back to me in 3D.

I had read more self development books in that year, than in my entire lifetime and my hunger for knowledge keeps growing. Some concepts were not easy to understand at first, and changing old habits into new took time, but with persistence I succeeded. I have reached a point where I realized that *true self* knows no limits: that in truth I can have, do, or be, virtually anything I desire to be.

I became an observer of my thoughts, and I see what my point of attraction is.

New relationships formed, existing relationships transformed, new business opportunities appeared, and with them, new opportunities to do that which I most love to do – teach, mentor, and inspire in a whole new way. This was the first time in my life I was truly happy and felt light in my heart and soul.

"Nothing has any power over me other than that which I give it through my conscious thoughts." ~Anthony Robbins

---

Living in alignment with my purpose

I invite each of you reading this to consider the hidden power of your mindset. All my results were the consequence of my mindset. When I set out to rebuild my life, I did not start with how. I started by looking inward and wondered, *what would I love?* I thought about what needed to be left in place, let go of, or learned anew.

I went through a great amount of inner healing and much of my sickness has dissolved. Best of all, my ability to communicate with others has improved dramatically, and I now connect with people around the world with joy and excitement.

By transforming my inner and outer world, I know I can help you do the same.

These negative concepts which you hold in your mind are obstructing the flow of energy which could, if it were given a chance to, breathe new life into you and into your results in life. Step out of your current comfort zone and give yourself permission to live a life that makes you feel excited to get out of bed every morning. Retaking control of yourself and changing from within can bring about a change in your immediate environment. Finally, you are powerful beyond measure with the capacity to make everlasting change that begins with you.

Amazing people showed up in my life and I joined mastermind groups to support me on my journey to what was possible. Find your people, explore a mastermind group, and begin your journey to a future that is worthy of who you are.

I now proudly host Book Study Club, coach, and mentor people from all over. I have created my own programs to teach and share my knowledge. The act of serving and focusing on others is the most rewarding experience I've encountered.

All of us have a story to tell, some deeper than others, but all equally important to the universe. My story has so many more layers, to be told another time.

Now I choose Love and Gratitude.

What would YOU Love?

Ewa Krempa

Ewa Krempa currently resides in Alberta, Canada.

She loves to travel and explore the world and has been to over fifty countries. Her life is full of colourful experiences, memories, and personal growth.

In leisure time, Ewa loves to spend time in nature, preferably by the ocean, reading and expanding her awareness, while raising her daughter and running her businesses.

Over the years, Ewa was privileged to meet Dr. Michael Bernard Beckwith, Dr. Wayne Dyer and Doreen Virtue and was always inspired by their spiritual teachings and growth. Dr. Dyer's quote remained with her over the years, "If you change the way you look at things, the things you look at change." While she had an interesting life, and many setbacks, she also had many hidden talents and abilities that she had not yet unleashed. A new mindset of moving forward was truly the catalyst that enabled her to experience and create what she has today.

Ewa is a devoted follower of Bob Proctor and Tony Robbins, as well as other great teachers thru out history. Her studies of multiple programs have helped her to create the world she dreamed of and now she helps her clients to do the same.

Now, Ewa is a founder & CEO of Dynamic Mindset Coaching, where she helps to mentor, coach and transform people's lives. She is a host of a weekly Book Study Club, other events, and has created her own programs as well. She loves seeing people become better versions of themselves mentally, physically, spiritually, financially, emotionally, and more.

Connect with Ewa https://www.linktr.ee/EwaKrempa.

CHAPTER 7

Half Time - Change of Field Side

by Gabriela Silberhorn

The sun was shining on my face. A light breeze stroked my cheeks. I breathed in the fresh air of February and let my gaze glide over the picturesque landscape that spread out before me. I was on the top of a 250-meter-high hill known as Walberla in Franconian, Switzerland in Germany. According to its history, the Walberla was a powerful place, where in earlier times ancient customs and rituals, such as solstice fires, were celebrated. It is a sport climbing rock, which due to its south-facing position, was a suitable rock for climbing on sunny days in winter. A small chapel adorned a gently sloping plateau to the north at the top of the hill. Toward the southwest directly above the climbing walls, which ranged from 30 to 50 meters high, stood a summit cross.

"Wonderful," I thought, enjoying the view. With 13 degrees Celsius and pure sun, it was relatively warm for mid-February. This prompted me and some of my friends to open the outdoor climbing season. Due to the mid-day sun, the rock was warm enough that my fingers no longer became numb from the cold.

At the end of the day, I had separated myself from our troop and hiked alone the remaining 50 meters up to the summit cross. I wanted to make a decision. Where could I do that better than at this place of power? A place where the forces and energies of nature were well-disposed towards us humans. I sat down on the bench by the cross and let my gaze wander into the distance.

In a few days, my 50th birthday was going to be knocking on the door. I sighed. It wasn't the age that was on my mind. I could look back on 50 fulfilling years with a smile. With many challenges, but colorfully authentic and real. I had lived it as best I could. Not always as I would have liked. But I had reconciled myself to that. From that point of view, I could use the already 50 years as a source of strength for the next 50 years. God willing. No, it was not the age. I often heard people say, "I don't feel like 50," but how should we know, how a person actually feels at 50? I was sitting there, and I didn't know how my life was going to go. That's what was giving me a headache.

Nine months earlier, I still had a plan. This included celebrating the middle of my life together with my husband, who was the same age, as a big event. His 50th birthday had been four months earlier in October. We had thought of having our annual Christmas party, with a few extras this time in addition to the band, which had been there every year. That would have been perfect timing right in the middle, between our birthdays. At least that was my wish.

But as the saying goes, if you want to make God laugh, make plans. Life had a different idea of perfect timing. And a different plan for me.

My husband had been reorienting since last April the year before. Which I found out at the end of May. The new orientation was called Claudia. That made all other plans moot for the time being. I had a hard time behind me.

56

Something like this only happens to others. At least that's what you think. For me it had been clear, if he wants to follow this reorientation further, our ways separate. I could not look away. And I didn't want to. Not anymore. Until then, I had suspected for a long time that something like this would come. And for half a year I had been praying for the truth. As a woman, you feel something like this, when you want to feel it. My attempts to bring the relationship back in a common direction had failed. We had gotten stuck. I had been struggling for years with health issues that severely limited me and kept pushing me to my limits. But they also allowed me to grow. In April, he had confirmed to me that everything was fine for him, that he had come to terms and was content. I had mentioned that I had the feeling that we were losing each other. In retrospect, I realized that, at this time, he had already resigned. And at this point, he had met Claudia while climbing. Life had taken his statement as an opportunity to act. It was of the opinion that for both of us, it should not continue to go on like this.

Two weeks later, in early June, he moved out.

I sat up here under the summit cross and thought about my new orientation. Gratitude rose up in me. I got through the first deep valley after the separation. Free fall and yet found ground under my feet again. I had remained upright. Honest with myself. For the last few weeks, I felt better, at least, so that I could be part of the climbing. When, in June, my world had collapsed, I had not thought that I would ever again feel the joy of life that comes from climbing in connection with the rock.

I had resolved, while up here, to decide what I was going to do on my 50th birthday. Nothing? Like all the years before when I helped organize my husband's birthdays or the Christmas party, but preferred to skip my birthday? Just not be the center of attention? And just not take the risk that no one would come to me?

Or was it time? Time to step out of the shadow in which I had voluntarily placed myself for years. I was queasy at the thought. But of course, coming out of my shadowy hiding place also meant taking responsibility for myself and my life. In some situations, I had been happy to hide behind my husband. There, if I failed, I could have told myself, "Well, it wasn't me who was the reason." If I hosted the celebration, I would be the center of attention! Then it was a matter of facing the possibility of failure. Failure that held the confirmation of my deeply hidden beliefs of, "No one wants me, no one will come to me, and it won't be good." My ex-husband had made it visible to all. At least that was my conviction about myself, that washed to the surface inside me. "I wasn't good enough, that's why nobody wants me, that's why he changed his orientation." Now I had a choice. Did I keep the stamp I had put on myself from old imprints, or was it time? Time for a change? Time to wake up!

Meanwhile, I was old enough. Half time, if I should reach my goal to make the 100 years in this life full. Perfect timing for a change of sides on the playing field of life. Running in the other direction. Bringing new perspectives into view. And score a few goals.

It made me smile. It fit my zodiac sign - Pisces with Gemini ascendant. The Pisces; sensitive, reserved, wait, and see. Combined with the Gemini; communicative and soaring to lofty heights. I'm no astrologer, but I was once told that the Ascendant takes over in the second half of life. I liked the idea. "Express both aspects, become whole," came to mind. Professionally, I had already lived out communication as a trainer for years. There, my belief system only made itself felt in a limited way. There, I could hold on to the system of my employer. Now it was time to put down the crutches and learn to walk and stand freely.

I looked into the slowly setting sun. I closed my eyes. No one but me is up here right now. Silence, broken only by the jingling of the carabiners, surrounded me.

I felt into my heart. Deep inside me, a rising joy stirred. "Do it," the feeling seemed to say. "Just do it and don't keep thinking about how it's going to be. It will be good. Do it!"

I opened my eyes. "Yes! I'm celebrating my 50th birthday in four days." Turning point! Almost 40 people I wanted to invite. I had briefly added that up this morning. Excitement was rising in me. My doubter spoke up. "You're crazy! How should that go in four days, a celebration with almost 40 people? But well, there probably won't be that many anyway. Nobody has time at such short notice." I watched my thoughts and smiled. So, I could at least tell myself again that it's not because of me that no one is coming, but that no one has time so shortly before. Even if no one would prepare something for my round birthday, I could blame it on this circumstance.

I pushed the doubter aside. Anything was better than nothing. This thought reduced my fear of failure a bit more.

I returned to my climbing group at the base of the wall. "The decision has been made!" I announced. "There will be a celebration on Thursday. No presents! Just bring something to eat and drink for the celebration if you want to come."

I sent out all the invitations via WhatsApp. The last **send** gave me palpitations. What had I done? In addition to my daily work, getting the house ready for lots of guests had me spinning my wheels a bit for the remaining four days. Due to the non-existent time, my perfectionism was completely overwhelmed. But that was also good! Thus, I could not think much about how it would be. What could go wrong? What could I do to make it good?

On Thursday, the time had come. Everyone came except for three friends who were on skiing vacation. 35 guests. My belief system shrunk 35 more times. There was enough to eat, there was a place for everyone, there was singing for me and with me, laughter, poetry and composing my own song for me. It was MY turning point!

A successful party. Inspired, I fell into bed at a late hour. Now I know, besides sensitive and deep diving, I can do that too, if I want to. I had washed the stamp off my forehead. At least this one.

Over the next few years, I continued to explore which stamps fit me better. There were some new ones. But also a few old ones remained faithful to me. Many things had already been good. Now it is perfectly imperfect. Everything may be. And in the course of the rest of my life, I will add a stamp, "Everything is possible." You just have to wake up.

It will take a while before I'm fully awake. There is still potential for development. But hopefully, I still have 44 years until the 100 are full!

When I look at the pictures and videos of this birthday on my phone, gratitude flows through my heart. So often, there is something good in everything that happens to us. Even if it brings down the foundational walls and it feels like you are losing the ground under your feet. Life keeps reaching out to you and holding your hand until you feel your footing again.

Life loves you ~ Louise L. Hay

So beautifully said. I can't always believe that, but I do so more and more often.

60

New challenges are currently accompanying my life's journey. Nobody can take this turning point away from me. Nor what I was allowed to experience in the years after. I experienced a change of perspective. Often the people who challenge and hurt you the most are your greatest teachers and guardian angels. And they open up new paths for you with possibilities that were previously undreamed of.

Everything is possible. It really is. But maybe that's not what it's all about. Maybe it's just about arriving at yourself through all the possibilities that life offers you. To become whole. At least I have come a little closer to that.

Gabriela Silberhorn

Gabriela Silberhorn grew up in beautiful Bavaria, Germany, where she still lives.

Due to her own challenges, life led her back deeper and deeper into the connection to the heart. Who am I and who do I want to be? Two questions that have preoccupied her since the age of 12 and have accompanied her throughout her life. Now, at the age of over 50, she is beginning to recreate herself once again, to develop new potential and to redefine her values and her orientation in life. As a trained banker, she currently supports her boss in his medium-sized company in the healthcare sector as a coach and personnel developer for their employees, as well as in the areas of finance and marketing. In her own small business, she offers spiritual art in the form of acrylic paintings such as mandalas, energy, and angel paintings and also mandala stones. Her artistic and creative vein was laid in her cradle by her parents. This gift also helps her in daily life and in her job to find creative solutions. New in her life is the writing work as an author. She has started authoring a new book in the form of a novel to express her life story and insights in a light and entertaining form. A new experience is also to write in English and not in her native German.

Her vision is to help people reconnect with their heart and intuition to live a fuller and happier life, despite all our earthly challenges.

Connect with Gabriela at www.energieundengelwelt.de.

CHAPTER 7A

Halbzeit - Wechsel der Feldseite

by Gabriela Silberhorn
(German version)

Die Sonne schien mir ins Gesicht. Eine leichte Brise streichelte meine Wangen. Ich atmete die frische Luft des Februars ein und ließ meinen Blick über die malerische Landschaft gleiten, die sich vor mir ausbreitete. Ich befand mich auf dem Gipfel eines 250 Meter hohen Hügels, der als Walberla in der Fränkischen Schweiz in Deutschland bekannt ist. Seiner Geschichte nach war das Walberla ein Kraftort, an dem in früheren Zeiten uralte Bräuche und Rituale wie Sonnwendfeuer gefeiert wurden. Es ist ein Sportkletterfelsen, der sich aufgrund seiner südlichen Lage auch an sonnigen Tagen im Winter zum Klettern eignete. Eine kleine Kapelle schmückte ein sanft abfallendes Plateau im Norden auf der Spitze des Hügels. Im Südwesten, direkt über den 30 bis 50 Meter hohen Kletterwänden, stand ein Gipfelkreuz.

"Wunderbar," dachte ich und genoss die Aussicht. Mit 13 Grad Celsius und Sonne pur war es für Mitte Februar relativ warm. Das hatte mich und einige meiner Freunde dazu veranlasst, die Outdoor-Klettersaison zu eröffnen. Durch die Mittagssonne war der Fels so warm, dass meine Finger nicht mehr von der Kälte taub wurden.

Am Ende des Tages hatte ich mich von unserer Truppe getrennt und war allein die restlichen 50 Meter bis zum Gipfelkreuz gewandert. Ich wollte eine Entscheidung treffen. Wo könnte ich das besser tun als an diesem Ort der Kraft. Ein Ort, an dem die Kräfte und Energien der Natur uns Menschen wohlgesonnen waren. Ich setzte mich auf die Bank neben dem Kreuz und ließ meinen Blick in die Ferne schweifen.

In ein paar Tagen würde mein 50. Geburtstag an die Tür klopfen. Ich seufzte. Es war nicht das Alter, das mich beschäftigte. Ich konnte mit einem Lächeln auf 50 erfüllte Jahre zurückblicken. Mit vielen Herausforderungen, aber farbenfroh, authentisch und echt. Ich hatte sie gelebt, so gut ich konnte. Nicht immer so, wie ich es mir gewünscht hätte. Doch damit hatte ich mich ausgesöhnt. So gesehen, konnte ich die vergangenen 50 Jahre als Kraftquelle für die nächsten 50 Jahre nutzen. So Gott will. Nein, es war nicht das Alter. Ich höre Menschen oft sagen: "Ich fühle mich nicht wie 50," aber woher sollen wir wissen, wie sich ein Mensch mit 50 tatsächlich fühlt? Ich saß da und wusste nicht, wie mein Leben weitergehen sollte. Das bereitete mir Kopfschmerzen.

Neun Monate zuvor hatte ich noch einen Plan. Dazu gehörte, die Mitte meines Lebens gemeinsam mit meinem gleichaltrigen Mann als großes Ereignis zu feiern. Sein 50. Geburtstag war vier Monate zuvor im Oktober gewesen. Wir hatten daran gedacht, unsere jährliche Weihnachtsfeier zu veranstalten, diesmal mit ein paar Extras zusätzlich zu der Band, die jedes Jahr dabei war. Das wäre das perfekte Timing gewesen, genau in der Mitte, zwischen unseren Geburtstagen. Zumindest war das mein Wunsch.

Aber wie man so schön sagt: Wenn du Gott zum Lachen bringen willst, mache Pläne. Das Leben hatte eine andere Vorstellung von perfektem Timing. Und einen anderen Plan für mich.

Mein Mann hatte sich seit April des vergangenen Jahres neu orientiert. Was ich Ende Mai herausfand. Die Neuorientierung hieß Claudia. Das machte alle anderen Pläne vorerst hinfällig. Ich hatte eine harte Zeit hinter mir.

So etwas passiert eigentlich immer nur anderen. Denkt man zumindest. Für mich war klar gewesen, wenn er dieser Neuorientierung weiter folgen will, trennen sich unsere Wege. Ich konnte nicht wegschauen. Und ich wollte es auch nicht. Nicht mehr. Bis dahin hatte ich schon lange geahnt, dass so etwas kommen kann. Und ein halbes Jahr lang hatte ich um die Wahrheit gebetet. Als Frau fühlst du so etwas, wenn du es fühlen willst. Meine Versuche, die Beziehung wieder in eine gemeinsame Richtung zu bringen, waren gescheitert. Wir hatten uns festgefahren. Ich hatte jahrelang mit gesundheitlichen Problemen zu kämpfen, die mich stark einschränkten und mich immer wieder an meine Grenzen brachten. Aber sie erlaubten mir auch, zu wachsen. Im April hatte er mir bestätigt, dass für ihn alles in Ordnung war, dass er sich damit abgefunden hatte und zufrieden war. Ich hatte erwähnt, dass ich das Gefühl hatte, dass wir uns gegenseitig verlieren würden. Im Nachhinein war mir klar geworden, dass er zu diesem Zeitpunkt bereits resigniert hatte. Und in dieser Zeit war er Claudia beim Klettern begegnet. Das Leben hatte seine Aussage zum Anlass genommen, zu handeln. Es war der Meinung, dass es für uns beide so nicht weitergehen sollte.

Zwei Wochen später, Anfang Juni, zog er aus.

Ich saß hier oben unter dem Gipfelkreuz und dachte über meine Neuorientierung nach. Dankbarkeit stieg in mir auf. Ich hatte das erste tiefe Tal nach der Trennung überwunden. Freier Fall und doch wieder Boden unter meinen Füßen gefunden. Ich war aufrecht geblieben. Aufrichtig zu mir selbst. Seit ein paar Wochen ging es mir besser, zumindest so weit, dass ich beim Klettern wieder dabei sein konnte. Als im Juni meine Welt gefühlt zusammengebrochen war, hätte ich nicht gedacht, dass ich jemals wieder die Lebensfreude spüren würde, die beim Klettern in Verbindung mit dem Felsen entsteht.

Ich hatte mir vorgenommen, während ich hier oben war, zu entscheiden, was ich an meinem 50. Geburtstag machen würde. Nichts? Wie in all den Jahren zuvor, als ich die Geburtstage meines Mannes oder die Weihnachtsfeier mitorganisierte, aber meinen Geburtstag lieber ausließ? Nur um nicht im Mittelpunkt zu stehen? Und nur nicht das Risiko eingehen, dass niemand zu mir kommen würde?

Oder war es an der Zeit? Zeit, aus dem Schatten herauszutreten, in den ich mich jahrelang freiwillig gestellt hatte. Mir war mulmig bei dem Gedanken. Aber klar, aus meinem Schattenversteck heraus zu kommen hieß auch, die Verantwortung für mich und mein Leben zu übernehmen. Bei einigen Situationen hatte ich mich gerne hinter meinem Mann versteckt. Dort hätte ich mir bei einem Scheitern gut einreden können, „War ja nicht ich der Grund!" Wenn ich die Feier ausrichten würde, würde ich im Mittelpunkt stehen! Dann hieß es, der Möglichkeit des Scheiterns ins Auge zu blicken. Ein Scheitern, das die Bestätigung meiner tief versteckten Glaubenssätze „mich will keiner, zu mir kommt keiner und es wird nicht gut" aufrecht hielt. Mein Ex-Mann hatte es für alle sichtbar gemacht. Zumindest war das meine Überzeugung über mich selbst, die in mir an die Oberfläche gespült worden war. "Ich war nicht gut genug, deshalb will mich keiner, deshalb hat er sich umorientiert." Jetzt hatte ich die Wahl. Wollte ich den Stempel behalten, den ich mir durch alte Prägungen aufgedrückt hatte, oder war es an der Zeit? Zeit für eine Veränderung? Zeit zum Aufwachen!

Inzwischen war ich alt genug. Halbzeit, wenn ich mein Ziel erreichen sollte, die 100 Jahre in diesem Leben voll zu machen. Perfektes Timing für einen Seitenwechsel auf dem Spielfeld des Lebens. In die andere Richtung zu laufen. Neue Perspektiven ins Blickfeld rücken. Und ein paar Tore erzielen.

Das brachte mich zum Lächeln. Es passte zu meinem Sternzeichen - Fische mit Aszendent Zwillinge. Die Fische sind sensibel, zurückhaltend und abwartend. Kombiniert mit dem Zwilling, der kommunikativ ist und sich in luftige Höhen aufschwingt. Ich bin kein Astrologe, aber mir wurde einmal gesagt, dass der Aszendent in der zweiten Lebenshälfte die Führung übernimmt. Die Idee hat mir gefallen. "Beide Aspekte ausdrücken, ganz werden," kam mir in den Sinn. Beruflich hatte ich die Kommunikation bereits jahrelang als Trainerin ausgelebt. Dort machte sich mein Glaubenssystem nur in begrenztem Maße bemerkbar. Dort konnte ich mich am System meines Arbeitgebers festhalten. Jetzt war es an der Zeit, die Krücken abzulegen und zu lernen, frei zu gehen und zu stehen.

Ich schaute in die langsam untergehende Sonne. Ich schloss meine Augen. Niemand außer mir war in diesem Moment hier oben. Stille, die nur durch das Klirren der Karabiner unterbrochen wurde, umgab mich.

Ich fühlte in mein Herz. Tief in mir regte sich eine aufsteigende Freude. "Tu es," schien das Gefühl zu sagen. "Tu es einfach und denke nicht darüber nach, wie es sein wird. Es wird gut sein. Tu es!"

Ich öffnete meine Augen. "Yes! In vier Tagen feiere ich meinen 50sten Geburtstag. Wendepunkt! Fast 40 Leute wollte ich einladen. Das hatte ich heute Morgen kurz zusammengezählt. Die Aufregung stieg in mir auf. Mein Zweifler meldete sich zu Wort. "Du bist verrückt! Wie soll das denn in vier Tagen gehen, eine Feier mit fast 40 Leuten? Aber gut, so viele werden es wahrscheinlich sowieso nicht sein. So kurzfristig hat niemand Zeit." Ich beobachtete meine Gedanken und lächelte. So konnte ich mir wenigstens wieder einreden, es liegt nicht an mir, dass niemand kommt, sondern daran, dass niemand so kurz vorher Zeit hat. Selbst wenn keiner etwas für meinen runden Geburtstag vorbereiten würde, könnte ich es auf diesen Umstand schieben.

Ich schob den Zweifler beiseite. Alles war besser als Nichts. Dieser Gedanke verringerte meine Angst vor dem Scheitern noch ein Stück mehr.

Ich kehrte zu meiner Klettergruppe am Wandfuß zurück. "Die Entscheidung ist gefallen!" verkündete ich. "Am Donnerstag gibt es eine Feier. Keine Geschenke! Bringt einfach etwas zu essen und zu trinken für die Feier mit, wenn ihr kommen wollt."

Ich verschickte alle Einladungen über WhatsApp. Beim letzten Senden bekam ich Herzklopfen. Was hatte ich nur getan? Zusätzlich zu meiner täglichen Arbeit musste ich in den verbleibenden vier Tagen das Haus für die vielen Gäste herrichten. Aufgrund der nicht vorhandenen Zeit war mein Perfektionismus völlig überfordert. Aber das war auch gut so. So konnte ich nicht viel darüber nachdenken, wie es sein würde. Was könnte schief gehen? Was sollte ich tun, damit es gut wird?

Am Donnerstag war es dann so weit. Alle kamen, bis auf drei Freunde, die im Skiurlaub waren. 35 Gäste. Mein Glaubenssystem schrumpfte 35mal ein bisschen mehr. Es gab genug zu essen, es gab einen Platz für alle, es wurde für mich und mit mir gesungen, gelacht, gedichtet und ein eigenes Lied für mich komponiert. Es war ein Wendepunkt für mich!

Eine gelungene Party. Beseelt fiel ich zu später Stunde ins Bett. Jetzt wusste ich, dass ich neben einfühlsam und tief tauchen auch das kann, wenn ich will. Ich wusch mir den Stempel von der Stirn. Zumindest diesen.

In den nächsten Jahren erkundete ich weiter, welche Stempel besser zu mir passten. Es gab einige neue. Aber auch ein paar alte blieben mir treu. Vieles war schon gut gewesen. Jetzt ist es perfekt unperfekt. Alles darf sein. Und im Laufe meines Lebens werde ich mir vielleicht einen Stempel aufdrücken: "Alles ist möglich." Du musst nur aufwachen.

Es wird wohl noch eine Weile dauern, bis ich ganz wach bin. Es gibt noch Entwicklungspotenzial. Aber ich habe ja hoffentlich noch 44 Jahre, bis die 100 voll sind!

Wenn ich mir die Bilder und Videos von diesem Geburtstag auf meinem Handy anschaue, durchströmt Dankbarkeit mein Herz. So oft steckt in allem, was uns widerfährt, etwas Gutes. Selbst wenn es die Grundmauern zum Einsturz bringt und es sich anfühlt, als würde man den Boden unter den Füßen verlieren. Das Leben reicht dir immer wieder die Hand und hält deine so lange fest, bis du wieder festen Boden unter den Füßen hast.

Das Leben liebt dich - Louise L. Hay

So schön gesagt. Nicht immer kann ich das glauben, aber immer öfter.

Neue Herausforderungen begleiten derzeit meine Lebensreise. Diesen Wendepunkt kann mir niemand mehr nehmen. Auch nicht das, was ich in den Jahren danach erleben durfte. Ich habe einen Perspektivenwechsel erlebt. Oft sind die Menschen, die dich am meisten herausfordern und verletzen, deine größten Lehrer und Schutzengel. Und eröffnen dir neue Wege mit Möglichkeiten, die du dir vorher nicht vorstellen konntest.

Alles ist möglich. Das ist es wirklich. Aber vielleicht geht es gar nicht darum. Vielleicht geht es nur darum, durch all die Möglichkeiten, die das Leben dir bietet, bei dir selbst anzukommen. Ganz zu werden. Dem bin ich zumindest ein Stück nähergekommen.

CHAPTER 8

Finding Confirmation and Faith in a Most Unexpected Place

by Janis F. Kearney

It was 1995 when I truly realized God's wicked sense of humor. At the same time, I knew that in the end He would only ask of me what He knew I could do. I just had to trust He wouldn't let me fail. I was forty-two years old, middle aged by American standards, the year that He presented me with a miracle, to take or not to take. I took it, and in 1995, I became a member of President William J. Clinton's oval office staff. I shouldn't get ahead of myself. There is always a backstory and for certain I had one.

I did not fit the profile of those who usually ended up in the place God placed me in 1995. Mine was not a storybook life. My parents were neither monied nor connected but were poor sharecroppers. Their claim to fame down in southeast Arkansas, was their nineteen children who were all good Christians, hard workers, and usually the top students in their classes in spite of the fact that many times they were kept out of school to finish that last bale of cotton.

The Kearney family's day-to-day lives, like most other families in our community, consisted of hard work. Our community was truly a village, made up of other sharecroppers, field laborers, small farmers and lots of children. In 1959, Daddy built our home on two acres of land. He'd saved up for years to ensure that Mama would celebrate Christmas in her own home that year.

Between 1971 and 1987, I finished undergraduate studies at the University of Arkansas, married, had a child, and embarked on a graduate degree that I never completed. Instead, I took a management job in Arkansas state government as an assistant program manager for a federal program, and later as a public information director for Migrant Education.

In 1987, God decided to shake things up in my life. One that would force me to grow more than I knew I could. Just like that, I left state government and was hired by Arkansas' civil rights legend Daisy Gatson Bates to be her managing editor at the revived Arkansas State Press, once the most recognized African American newspaper in the south.

I served as managing editor for the newspaper for all of three months, before Mrs. Bates walked into the office on a bright autumn morning and beckoned me to her desk. When the beautiful, but visibly ailing publisher asked me to sit, I could sense sorrow on her face. She reached for my hands and held them as she told me she was retiring and selling the newspaper.

I went home that evening devastated and angry. Was the anger directed at God, who lured me from my "good" state job, for a role that lasted three months? In truth, I realized, He was pushing me to take on the reins of the newspaper. Was He serious? I soon realized my only option would be to become an unemployment statistic. I prayed for the next two days, and finally went in and asked Daisy Bates to sell her newspaper to me. I'd be darned if I'd let God think I couldn't handle the challenge!

Amazingly, Daisy Bates looked me straight in the eye and nodded. "I think you got the fire in the belly to take over this newspaper." I've yet to receive a compliment as life changing as that one sentence. Most importantly, she sold the newspaper to me with the knowledge that I could only pay her half of her asking price up front. I paid the balance over the next two years.

I fell in love with newspaper publishing though I swear it was the hardest job I've ever had. I kept telling myself I was doing what God wanted me to do and what Daisy Bates believed I could do. For another five years, I basked in the community's awe of a younger female publisher of what was once the most recognized black newspaper this side of the Mississippi.

By 1992, I had arrived at a comfort zone at the newspaper, and the community had finally accepted me as a legitimate newspaper publisher. I was enjoying the role and learning so much about the community, the leadership, and politics, something that had never really interested me. The summer of 1992, however, would mark another huge pivot for me. I was asked to join the Clinton-Gore Presidential campaign. I knew and liked Governor Clinton, and decided I'd like to help him in his run for president.

I took a sabbatical from my newspaper, turning over the day-to-day operation to my managing editor. I worked as the campaign's minority media coordinator during the day and returned to my newspaper for a few hours each night. I was overjoyed when Governor Clinton won in the general election. Yes, the campaign had been exciting, but I was also excited to return to my newspaper and work full-time.

Who coined the phrase, 'nothing lasts forever?' After Governor William Jefferson Clinton won the election for President, guess who was asked to join the white house staff? My final decision to say "yes" led to other changes: leaving my 89-year-old father whom I'd grown so close to after my mother's death ten years earlier, carting my son off to Morehouse College for his freshman year, knowing I wouldn't be able to be there for him as I'd always envisioned I would. The scariest part was leaving Arkansas for the first time in my life.

These were not the only life-changing things to happen around that time. Two years earlier, my husband of sixteen years, and I, divorced. We'd been college sweethearts who married too young for the wrong (or right) reason—our son who was now a freshman in college. God was probably laughing his head off, knowing my plans and my reality were light years apart.

Off I went to Washington, DC., as green as they come. Knowing absolutely nothing about the national political culture. Afraid of all the boogiemen I'd been warned about by friends and foes. It took me a year to realize that the city has as much beauty, culture, and history as any part of the country. There was an energy in its vibe. I slowly but surely fell in love with my new home, this amazing city with its vibrant culture. I amazed myself when I became comfortably immersed in the governmental and political scenes.

When I'd arrived at the White House, I was placed in the office of Media Affairs, serving as a media specialist with focus on foreign, minority and religious press. By March, however, the President appointed me to the Small Business Administration as Public Communications Director. I loved the role and the people I worked with. I was able to use everything I'd learned about organizational communications and public affairs back in Arkansas, and more.

It was 1995, however, when my life truly changed. A miracle that would have me pinching myself every day for the next five years. Here was God, again, sending a new shockwave to my system. President Clinton in 1995, decided he wanted to hire an aide who would serve as part biographer, part historian—a personal diarist to the President. Maybe more than any other U.S. President, Bill Clinton truly believed that the White House and the presidency belonged to the American people. My role represented that belief.

There came God again, telling me the job was designed for me... and there went awe-struck me, falling for it. I applied for the job, then went about my everyday work not really expecting to hear back. But I did hear back, a few months later. After a lengthy interview, I again decided it was just part of the process and they'd probably already chosen their applicant.

Another few weeks passed before I received a call from the oval office, the President wanted me to come in for a personal interview. God did it again, messed with me...I interviewed and shortly after was told I got the job. After my interview with the President, the oval office director told me my role was to chronicle the presidency, every day of the presidency, and document how the White House operated. This documentation would be for future Presidential historians, writers, biographers, students of presidential history. Me... a Personal Diarist to a President? It was something I would never have known to dream about, back on Varner Road.

Fascinating is hardly adequate to describe what it was like serving as the chronicler of the U.S. Presidency. Sitting in meetings with U.S. political leaders, congressional leaders, corporate and institutional leaders—each of them there to meet with the President. How many times did I witness men, women and children walk into the oval office to meet the President of the United States, for the first time. I saw world leaders blush and awkwardly greet the leader of the free world. I saw lifelong devotion blossom after one brief conversation. It was not only the excitement of meeting this particular President, but also the awesome power of the American Presidency that left many powerful men and women speechless.

I served in the role for almost six years, and never experienced a dull moment. I watched history being made before my eyes. I saw up close how men negotiated Americans' lives and the future of our nation, how they wrangled for hours deciding what was right or wrong for the rest of the world. I witnessed good politics, and bad. Good men and women who all likely came to their roles with good hearts and intentions. Some, however, fell prey to the drug of political power.

So, how did serving in the role of Personal Diarist to President Clinton change me? The opportunity humbled me, made me want to be a better version of myself. If I'd ever stopped dreaming, given up on hope, began believing that God sometimes forgot me, I committed to never allowing myself to believe that again. I remembered back to those long hot days of chopping cotton from morning until night, or picking cotton in the coldest of winter, or going to school without lunch money or the necessary books; even then I'd believed God watched over me, and that miracles were real. I now realize that life very often rains on our childlike beliefs, and makes it hard for us to believe in miracles. At forty years old, I was blessed with confirmation that miracles are real. I'd hold onto this belief, now, for the rest of my life.

Maybe that chapter of my life was indeed God testing me. The wonderful thing about that? He chose me for that test, and I was blessed beyond all expectations. At forty years old, I had been chosen for a role that the hundred-plus younger, smarter, prettier, and far more connected applicants would have given anything, for. This moment in my life, more than any other time, confirmed what my parents had tried instilling in us all their lives – keep doing what is right and good and don't let the world change you. This was confirmation of my parents' teachings, the values they instilled in each of us; the community philosophy I saw practiced each and every day, of giving back and doing your very best even if no one was watching.

I am thankful beyond words for that scary giant step He nudged me into taking. He was always there to catch me should I fall.

Janis F. Kearney

Janis F. Kearney is President and Founder of the Celebrate! Maya Project. She is an author, book publisher, and writing instructor, born to southeast Arkansas cotton sharecroppers. She attended Gould Public Schools and graduated from the University of Arkansas at Fayetteville with a B.A. in Journalism, after starting out in the English department. She served nine years as a project manager and public affairs director for the Arkansas state government. She served briefly as managing editor for civil rights legend Daisy L. Bates' historic <u>Arkansas State Press</u> Newspaper, before purchasing and becoming publisher of the newspaper in 1988, upon Bates' retirement. She served eight years in the Clinton administration, six of those years as President Clinton's Personal Diarist.

In 2001, she and her husband moved to Chicago where Janis began her writing life, eventually founding her small publishing company. Since that time, she has published seventeen books through her company. In 2014, she founded with the help of a small number of other women, the Celebrate! Maya Project a 501(c)(3) that honors the memory of Dr. Maya Angelou's life and legacy through work with youth in the Arkansas Delta through literacy, writing, poetry and art projects.

Janis is married to Bob J. Nash who served as President Clinton's Director of Presidential Personnel. They share three children and six grandchildren. Janis says she writes memoirs to remember, clarify, and share her world.

Learn more about Janis and her writing life and Celebrate! Maya Project at https://www.celebratemayaproject.org.

CHAPTER 9

An Educator Awakens

by Karen L. Haines

Every person is on a journey, their own personal journey with its ups and downs. Like many individuals, I have struggled with my path and have wondered what more there is to this life. Last year I was propelled into going through a mid-life awakening. While it has been challenging it has also been an important journey for me at this time in my life.

For me, things really came to a head in October of 2021 when I had what I would consider *a complete meltdown*. Now, I understand that I was in the throes of Post-Traumatic Stress Disorder (PTSD), which I had no idea I suffered from until I was pushed to the brink of not being able to function. I had been an educator and administrator for over thirty years in three states and multiple districts, and the cumulative stress had finally taken its toll. It was time for me to awaken to new possibilities.

In my case, even though I was concerned about the stigma of getting help, I decided to seek out a professional. I was in a really bad place and knew I needed assistance in order to start the healing and waking process. Some individuals may not need professional guidance, but in my particular situation I felt it was necessary.

When my *meltdown* occurred, I was holding a prominent position as an educational administrator and realized I had wrapped my entire identity into my career. I didn't know who I was. The only way I could describe myself was in relation to being an educator for thirty years. It was time for me to focus attention on myself, which was awkward for someone like me. I was used to focusing all my attention on others instead of attending to my own thoughts, desires and needs.

I had no idea the extent of the strain my career had placed on my mental and physical health, especially after suffering multiple student tragedies throughout my career that had caused the post-traumatic stress disorder. My PTSD was coupled with severe depression and anxiety. I was lost and unsure of what I wanted from my life, making the depression and anxiety even worse.

My body and mind had been slowly shutting down from the incredible daily stress of being an educator. It was time for me to take a ginormous step back to really look at myself and begin the hard work, the important work, of determining where I was in my life and how I wanted to move forward. How was I going to move ahead as a middle-aged woman that needed to find a new purpose and way of defining herself? My entire being and motivation in life had been as an educator and administrator up until that point. All I knew was wrapped up in giving all my energy to my students, parents, teachers, and community members. It was time for me to unravel what I believed about myself and how I identified my place in this world.

I found myself in a very scary, unnerving time of my life. I couldn't fathom what was next when all I had ever known as an adult was being an educator. I was pushed into a precarious situation where I left my career to focus on healing and learning more about who I was outside of education. It was time to discover myself, which was frightening.

Everyone has an individual journey and mine required intensive counseling to heal and begin to determine my next steps. That may not be everyone's path, but it's important for me to be open and honest as it might encourage other individuals that might be suffering to seek out professional help. Sometimes professional help is necessary to begin healing, and in my case, healing that I wasn't even aware I needed. I was just so accustomed to the daily stressors I encountered that they became a routine part of my life. That is, until I took that big step off the perpetual merry-go-round and took stock of my health and life.

As I began my own journey, I realized that it was okay to ask for help, which was a huge realization for someone that is very reluctant to ask for any assistance. I was used to being the strong administrator that others could rely upon. I wasn't accustomed to being the individual that required the support of and help from others. I was primed for a mid-life awakening in order to heal and move forward.

In addition to the professionals supporting me, I also began to read a variety of books. I found several focused-on meditation practices, specifically the most significant book that resonated with me was *Breaking the Habit of Being Yourself* by Dr. Joe Dispenza. After reading the book, I began my daily meditation practice. This was beneficial as I began to find my new path focused on healing and discovering my individual identity that wasn't completely wrapped up in being an educator. In addition, I began a daily yoga practice to help clear my mind and find ways to be present in every moment. I had to take a giant step back to really look at who I am and what I wanted out of life now. It was scary and intimidating, especially at my age. It was time to wake up and reinvent myself. Something I had always kind of thought of as a cliché. I understand now that it is alright to be at a place in life that forces us to look at things in a different light and with a new perspective. Both meditation and yoga helped me do that by training me to focus on the present.

Instead of having a mid-life crisis, I like to believe and focus on the more positive way of looking at it by having gone through a mid-life awakening. By definition, an awakening is *an act or moment of becoming suddenly aware of something*. While some aspects of my life felt like I was in crisis, other parts of me were excited about becoming more aware of my life, to begin a new journey - a journey without constraints and labels.

I felt as if I had suddenly woken up from a bad dream – a dream that I had completely built for myself until I was ready to wake up and begin to live my life in the present. Being in the present doesn't allow you to live in the past or in the future, which I was highly trained to do. Being present means being fully focused on what one is doing. I was ready to be awake and present in my life rather than going through the day-to-day motions that had been wrapped up in my career.

While I understand how intimidating and humbling a mid-life awakening may be. I personally am very happy to have woken up and stopped going through the routines that were so ingrained in me, routines that also caused tremendous stress and distress. Without going through a mid-life awakening, I never would have had the courage to start working on a book or developing a new prototype that is currently being patented. Both endeavors have allowed me to live my dream of being an author and inventor, two things I never would have moved forward with had I not been going through a mid-life awakening! Sometimes going through really tough times can bring forth new pathways, even those that you never believed possible.

It is scary to look at where you are, and then wake up—so you can begin to live life in the present, but the expedition is well worth it. I am tremendously grateful to have taken this new journey as my life feels much more fulfilling and joyful.

Karen Haines

Karen Haines loves being a mother to her 3 adult children: Kassidy, Kelston, and Keaghan as well as being a grandmother to Aurora. She is thrilled to have reconnected and now married to her lifelong friend and the love-of-her-life, Robert. Karen is passionate about her family and loves to spend time with them whenever possible.

Karen has been an educator for over 30 years in Alaska, Colorado, and Idaho where she resides with her husband now. Karen is also the president and founder of ElephantVision, an organization focused on helping children with vision tracking difficulties, which causes reading issues that are not addressed or treated in schools. In addition, Karen is a heartfelt supporter of the David Sheldrick Trust that rescues and rehabilitates elephants back into the wild.

Karen is working on publishing a book about her experiences as an educator in rural Alaska. In addition, Karen has been following her dream of developing and patenting a prototype of a product that will be launched this year. Both of her causes will be supported by the sales of her book and product.

Karen has a tremendous love for travel and desire to learn about and from other cultures. She travels as much as possible and hopes to visit more countries and states in the upcoming years.

Connect with Karen at www.elephantvision.org.

CHAPTER 10

The Evolution of Self: My Journey of Awakening and Growth through 25 Years of Midlife and Beyond

by Kathleen M. Tarochione

"I've never been sick a day in my life!," I used to boast with pride. But the truth is, my body has experienced its fair share of ailments and illnesses over the years. Despite that, my soul has grown and awakened beyond my wildest dreams. Looking back, I feel grateful for the person I've become today, knowing that no matter how much my health deteriorated, I never let it stop my spiritual growth.

Let me take you on a journey down memory lane and share my story. It was around twenty-five years ago, when I was fifty years old and feeling pretty good about myself. My husband-to-be and I were taking a stroll down Magnificent Mile in Chicago when I suddenly couldn't catch my breath. I wasn't significantly overweight, but I couldn't understand why I was so out of breath. It would take me years to uncover the reason behind my breathing difficulties.

In 2000, my husband, Tark, and I tied the knot. Shortly after our wedding, he began to feel unwell and ended up needing a double knee replacement. Despite the challenges we faced, taking care of "My Guy," as I lovingly called him, was an absolute pleasure. It was a chance for me to show my love and gratitude for all the years of happiness he brought into my life.

Tark's health journey was a challenging one. From surgery to rehab, to a walker, and then an electric scooter, his physical abilities were dwindling. Despite this, his doctor scolded him for not exercising enough, and little did I know, he was even sicker than we thought.

When Tark got sick, it was a shock to our systems. But we were determined to fight his illness together. I did everything in my power to take care of him, and I'm grateful we had some extra time together before he passed away. It was a difficult time, and I went through a period of grief that felt never-ending.

Life can be tough sometimes, and it can throw us curveballs that we never saw coming. I can relate to this on a personal level, as I've been through some challenging experiences in my life as well. But even in the face of adversity, I've learned that there's always a way to keep moving forward and find joy in life.

In our community, we had a lot of stray cats, and I was known as The Cat Lady for my animal advocacy work. One day, while assisting a momma cat with her birthing, I was bitten, resulting in a severe infection that led to a heart attack. The toll it took on me was significant, and Tark's health was deteriorating rapidly. Having Tark and I both needing assistance, it was beautiful to watch us take care of each other. Such a blended life. We were like two bodies in one.

After five years of uncertainty, we finally discovered the root cause of Tark's declining health—liver cancer. Unfortunately, the tumor was too large to operate on, and the prognosis was six to twelve months to live. I knew I had to do everything in my power to help him. I jumped into action, researching every healthy and spiritual alternative I could find. From essential oils to meditation, deep breathing, healthy eating plans, massages, and even laughter. I knew the power of energy to heal because of my spiritual beliefs. I made sure we went out every day with our dog named Maggie, finding solace in the little moments of joy.

To my surprise, Tark surpassed his prognosis and was still with me six to twelve months later. I was overjoyed and took care of him, our dog, and the feral cats in our community. He managed to live another five years, and I cherish every moment we had together. On July 29, 2010, Tark passed away peacefully in my arms. Even though he's no longer with me, he continues to live on in my heart and memories, and his love and spirit will never fade.

Eventually I found a way to channel my energy into something positive. My love for dogs and art led me to create Fine Art Creations for Dogs, which brought me a lot of joy. However, my health took a turn for the worse, and I was diagnosed with COPD. Losing my beloved dog Maggie was a blow to my spirit, but I found solace in Charlie, my Lhasa Apso mix, and in sharing my passion for dogs with others through The Dog Connection Show.

It seemed like every time I took a step forward, life would knock me back down again. Toxic mold in my house left me feeling sick, and I had to move to Phoenix, Arizona, where my health continued to be a struggle. But I kept pushing forward, determined to find a way to make a positive impact in the world.

When Colleen approached me with the opportunity to buy a home together, I was hesitant at first. I didn't know her very well, and it seemed like a risky proposition. But her passion for helping animals and incorporating my Dog Connection Show into her future plans convinced me to take a chance. It wasn't an easy decision, but I knew I had to keep moving forward and find ways to make a positive impact in the world, no matter what challenges came my way.

A month later, I arrived in Las Cruces, New Mexico, to my new home. I quickly realized I had made a mistake, as Colleen had three small dogs that were not housebroken, two cats, and another large dog that immediately started a fight with my Charlie. The odors were overwhelming, which posed a threat to my health condition and was a major trigger for COPD. Colleen isolated Charlie in "my area of the house" by putting a doggy door in my bedroom so he could go outside without coming through the house. Then, she put a 5'x7' dog run right outside the doggy door, which was all stones. Charlie, being almost fifteen years old, found it difficult to walk on the stones.

One of my biggest mistakes was opening a joint account with Colleen to pay the expenses, as I was paying for 50 percent of the mortgage, utilities, and groceries, but I was limited on how much access I would have to the house.

I didn't have access to the garage, which Colleen had used for her car and storage, and she had the master 30'x40' suite with a jacuzzi, walk-in shower, and outside private patio. In contrast, I had a 10'x10' bedroom with a 10'x10' for my office. I was limited to a 300 square-foot area in a 2,000 square-foot home, which indicated that Colleen was trying to oust me out of my own home.

After living uncomfortably in the house for almost a year, the stress finally got to me, and I was hospitalized again. When I got out of the hospital, I had a list of changes that needed to be made to the house, including keeping the temperature between 68–72 degrees, installing industrial HEPA Air Purifiers, additional high volume oxygen concentrators, and much more. I needed to put a door into my area to have total privacy and no dog hair, which was a significant issue for me. Colleen did not want to make any changes to the house and did not want to continue living with a person that required medical care.

Then, the sabotage began. Colleen started throwing out my food, emptying the ice machine, and refusing to turn on the air conditioning until it got to 86 degrees, knowing full well that I needed it at 72 degrees at the highest. I was still broadcasting my Dog Connection Show until Colleen deliberately changed our internet from high speed to basic. I hired an attorney who helped with a settlement, as I knew I needed to get out of the house but could not afford to move and pay a mortgage. I was willing to transfer the ownership of my home to Colleen through a Quitclaim deed, but she refused the settlement. However, she wanted me to move out of the house while continuing to pay the mortgage. As a result, I was forced to leave my home. Fortunately, I had the help of my attorney to make the move.

Unexpectedly, I received an email from Trina, a woman who had known Colleen for over fifteen years. Trina was planning to sue me due to my joint home ownership with Colleen and my role as an officer in Colleen's non-profit organization. This was the first time I had heard about it, and I was completely bewildered. To my surprise, I quickly became friends with Trina, and we worked together to uncover Colleen's fraudulent activities. We discovered that Colleen had been transferring money from her non-profit donation funds into our joint account to pay for the mortgage and other expenses. Moreover, Colleen used the EIDL grant money, which was intended for Covid relief, to pay for the down payment on the house. To make matters worse, Colleen had two outstanding Federal Tax Liens that she failed to disclose at the time of the mortgage loan.

I realized I was living with a criminal, and she was plotting to implicate me in her wrongdoing. I immediately went to the bank with the documents that proved Colleen's fraudulent activities. I filed a complaint with the police department and was referred to the District Attorney's office. The FBI later got involved in my case, and I provided a three-hour interview under oath. I had to act fast, and an Earth Angel kindly offered me a place to stay temporarily because I was now legally homeless. It was a terrifying experience.

In 2022, I ended up in the hospital twice due to life-threatening COPD, pneumonia, right-sided heart failure, pulmonary effusion, bradycardia, sepsis, and four exacerbations. My brother came to the hospital from San Clemente, California, to be with me and help me get my affairs in order. At that time, I had to say my goodbyes to my family and friends.

While I was in the hospital, I consulted my attorney, who advised me to file a Suit to Partition to force the sale of the house. Because of my fragile health, time was of the essence in case of my early demise. Eventually, I won the case, and my home is now up for sale. Unfortunately, the bank also colluded with Colleen, and I am now embroiled in a lawsuit with them, too.

Trina and I encountered some setbacks in life, but we used them as an opportunity to help other single, widowed, or divorced women who need support, just like I did. Together, we established the Golden Girls Community LLC, which aims to provide resources and assistance for women in similar situations.

Our revolutionary "Lifestyle" community offers a safe and empowering physical space for women to live independently while surrounded by a supportive network of like-minded individuals. In addition, we provide a virtual Golden Girls Connection, connecting women over fifty-five from all over the world to share experiences and grow together. Our mission is to create a community built on genuine connections and real-life experiences, fostering positive changes in our members' lifestyles.

Through my own personal experiences, spanning from my fifties to my mid-seventies, our community was designed to cater to a diverse range of issues women may face. From finding love, happiness, and financial stability to overcoming illness, dealing with loss, and even fraud or conspiracy, we offer support and resources to tackle any challenge. Our ultimate goal is to bring peace of mind to our members, which is something I myself am actively seeking.

The legacy of the Golden Girls is something I am immensely proud of. It serves as a testament to the fact that, even during a prolonged midlife crisis, it's possible to turn things around and create a positive impact. Our community is a place of compassion, empathy, and understanding, where women can come together to navigate the ups and downs of life with grace and dignity.

Kathleen Tarochione

Kathleen Tarochione is a Co-Founder/Partner at Golden Girls Community LLC. She is the owner of Picture A Moment Pet Productions LLC, a pet media production company.

She produces and co-hosts LIVE shows. She is nationally recognized as an on-air talent in the live streaming industry.

Kathy's passion is contributing to the well-being of others, so producing educational and community-based shows helps her accomplish her dreams.

As a Golden Girl herself, she desires to help those women who want to live a lifestyle with like-minded women have a meaningful and productive life.

Connect with Kathleen at https://www.goldengirlscommunity.com.

CHAPTER 11

A Journey to Possibility

by Katie Brennan

"Turn your wounds into wisdom." ~Oprah Winfrey

Peace, generosity, and joyful acceptance are daily pleasures I experience in this powerful chapter called mid-life. It has become a time of love and possibility – a time when the earlier, seemingly random dots of life are connecting to create the most beautiful image. It's not perfect, but that is part of the beauty - it's not supposed to be. My previously held expectation, that I would someday reach perfection, no longer exists. In fact, my previous constant drive for control and judgment of self and others has given way to a life that is more magical and promising than anything my younger self could have dreamed possible. I recognize that I have power over me - no one else. Without the need to control others, I am free to ride the wave of contentment that I hope will propel me forward for the rest of my life.

This life journey has morphed from being externally driven to a daily, moment-by-moment commitment to lead from my heart. I used to think the answers to life's mysteries were out there - in a partner, in my children, in nature. I believed that, somehow, others were blessed with knowledge and insights that I never received. It has taken years of examining and challenging the past to realize that the key to a fulfilling life rests within. Yes, there is still much that should be discovered and experienced in the outer world - nature, different cultures, music, and dance, but if my eyes cannot see and my heart cannot feel, all the beauty and love in the world will be for naught.

Chapter 1 was a childhood of not fitting in. And I was desperate to fit in, anywhere, at any cost. In my attempts to be part of the **in** crowd, poor choices and negative beliefs about myself landed me in many precarious situations. The prices I paid were certainly not ones I am proud of. In fact, most of my adult life was filled with shame and regret over choices made in childhood. Layer upon layer of masking created a child who fit in, but the cost was crippling.

Chapter 2, a blip in my journey, was a time of great wonder and expansion. It saw glimmers of acceptance, exploration and hope. But before this joy would settle in to become my current way of life, another chapter and thirty years of lessons would have to be experienced.

Chapter 3 was marked by years of insecurity, doubt and depression. The winter of 2014 is when it all came crashing down. As they say in AA, I hit rock bottom. I had just moved out from a toxic relationship, my young, unreachable son's violence had hit a dangerous level. Work was intolerable, my intermittent depression was full on and my overwhelmed mind simply shut down. Basic tasks became impossible. I could no longer read or think clearly. Simple conversations became challenging. Work and parenting switched to autopilot. The suicide meanies grabbed hold, convincing me that quitting life was the best option for everyone. Fortunately, my supports recognized the precipice I was blindly careening toward and got me into an inpatient program for women.

I was not new to counseling or introspection - weekly therapy had been an integral part of my life. Still, the introduction to **complex** PTSD (CPTSD) changed everything. It offered a possible alternative to the belief that I was born damaged goods. I learned that repeated, early childhood trauma resulted in a lifetime of thoughts, beliefs and behavioral patterns that were initially developed in response to overwhelming situations. Over time, these patterns intensified into **subconscious habits** that drove my life - I consistently responded to situations as if I was in danger even when I was not. My body reacted before my mind even knew what was happening. This new information led me to wonder, *what if I could quiet my body down enough to allow for thoughtful, more appropriate decisions?* Though this understanding was not quite that straightforward, it allowed true, deep healing to begin.

Recovery started in my mind, which was simultaneously my greatest asset and my worst enemy. I was blessed with an innate intelligence that allowed me to get through situations that were difficult for others. But it also filled me with relentless critical, judgmental, and self-sabotaging thoughts. Before my time in the hospital, it never occurred to me to challenge my thoughts as anything but the truth. Questioning the credibility of my mind, a seemingly simple act, opened in me a world of possibilities. The lifelong belief that I was a flawed human, destined to always be worthless, could be challenged. I could strip myself of that "truth" to create something completely different. I could get back to knowing that I, like everyone else, was born a precious, innocent soul, as powerful and deserving as everyone else.

At the time that these new and emotional awarenesses were taking place, I stumbled upon The Body Keeps the Score by Bessel Van Der

Kolk. It helped me understand how, in addition to storing trauma in my mind and thoughts, it had also been stored in my body. Therapy helped me understand my mind, but substantive changes could only occur once my body became an active participant in the healing process. Fortunately, I was a devout tai chi practitioner, so I was already aware of different body sensations. The calm state this practice produced had been its daily reward. With this new knowledge, tai chi became the starting place to relieve the body's traumatic memories.

I had trained to release tension in muscles, tendons and fascia to allow energy to flow naturally throughout my body. A curious new release presented itself in the healing of CPTSD - tears. I didn't exactly cry; tears just poured out of me, as if healing had a life of its own.

Slowly, I have learned to recognize and respond differently when there is an ache in my shoulder or in my heart. I am learning to **be** with it. To stop fighting it. To stop wishing it were different. Just acknowledge its existence. I let my mind focus on the tension and just observe it. Give it the attention it is begging for, much the way a loving mom can't fix a scraped knee, but can cuddle with the crying child until the pain has dissipated enough that she is ready to go off to play again, while the body instinctually heals the wound. It is not a question of mental will, release happens because there is a body intelligence that is far wiser and quicker than anything my mind can conceive of. Let the wisdom of my body heal the wound. When I can accept the pain instead of resisting it then follow that with curiosity and patience, the pain actually goes away.

It seems completely counterintuitive - I don't like discomfort, I want it to go away. Every part of me screams **DO something**. My mind rushes to avoid pain. Physical, emotional, mental, it doesn't matter which - an ache in my body is as intolerable as a judgmental thought about who I am. Both set off a series of habituated reactions stemming from a past filled with doubt and fear. When those thoughts get the better of me, my mind can spin on any number of repeated, self-deprecating stories. When I am perceptive enough to recognize when this is happening, I can **stop**. Observe. Let go of judgment. Once I can see, feel and accept what is happening, options present themselves. I can make wise, life-positive choices.

Alleviating the physical pain was one thing. Quieting my mind required more patience and effort. Layers and years of painful, intermingling thoughts made pinpointing specific culprits more complicated. I'm too... or I'm not... are two of my common critiques. Fortunately, positive results in the physical realm paved the way for non-judgmental awareness and acceptance of whatever comes to my mind. As with the body, objectivity is the key when dealing with thoughts. I begin with recognition of the thought, no matter how unpleasant or disturbing. Then I stop. Just observe it, allow whatever arises to just be. And here's the really hard part... **Don't rush to think of something different, in an effort to avoid whatever feeling comes with it. Feel it.** It is difficult to face that I have such disturbing thoughts. Untangling judgments and thoughts have been like patiently unraveling a mile of knotted twine. I have moments of success followed by weeks of backsliding. But the overall trend is upward.

The answer to pain is so simple. On paper, it sounds so easy. Be patient. Accept. Trust. But this is the hardest work I have ever done.

Once the shift to allow the wisdom of my mind and body to emerge, the next logical step was to take a deep, hard look at my behaviors. What was working for me? That is, what would I like to keep, moving forward, and what was time to let go of?

Just as I was becoming aware of the malleability of my physical aches and thoughts, divine intervention led me to a Feminine Power program. With a group of like-minded women, and a sense of belonging, another dimension was added to my inward journey. **Spirit.** I finally understand that I am more than just my mind and body. Together my mind, body, and soul are coalescing to create an awakened midlife. Life, I now know, is so much bigger than my little being.

There will always be skills to learn, actions to practice, beliefs to uncover and work to be done. Sounds crazy, but I have had to learn simple things like how to apologize and ask for forgiveness. History taught me to run from situations where a simple, genuine apology could have preserved a relationship. I continue to discover the distorted stories I tell myself and can better discern how well they do or do not match up with current reality. I am learning that I really am not alone and that my heart is much happier when I have a deeply vulnerable conversation with a trusted friend. I can be kind to others, at no cost to me, and new deeper relationships can emerge.

It is a daily, almost minute-by-minute, decision to respond from a place of greater good for all. That means I spend time every morning making sure that I exercise, set a loving intention for the day, reflect on the previous day and decide what I could have done differently or better. I have to make sure to eat well and get plenty of sleep. It is making the effort to connect with my supportive community every day, to remember that I matter to others and that they matter to me. Reminders that I am not just floating out in the universe alone mean that I check in with my children and grandchildren regularly. Each practice tips the scale towards joy, but it is the collective discipline that brings about a life full of possibilities, connection, love, and peace.

Now, in this, the 4th chapter, I wake up hopeful and excited to see what the day will bring. I am learning to limit expectations, so that I can be present with whatever arises. My commitment is to do my best to live from joy and love in mind, body and spirit. One choice at a time.

I accept that I am not going to wake up one day having arrived. I have already arrived, this is it. This one precious moment. When I let divine love guide me, I act in ways that are loving and generous.

Internal transformation is a funny thing. On the outside, I look the same. Okay, there are a few more pounds and many more wrinkles. On the inside, however, the gift of these practices, which have united my mind, body, spirit, is nothing short of a miracle.

Katie Brennan

Katie Brennan is a mom, a grandma, a teacher, a lover of life, an author, a coach, but mostly an ever-evolving woman. She has been married and divorced, birthed children and launched them, built a career and retired, lived overseas and in the states, in poverty and in financial abundance, battled cancer, survived, experienced trauma and recovered to flourish. She finds inspiration from the outdoors, always in search of her next creative endeavor.

Katie's first career as a public school teacher enabled her to design, develop, and teach a program in innovation and design based on the Stanford Design Model. She is now in love with her second career. As a coach for middle aged women who have given to others for most of their lives, she helps her clients step into their own dreams and desires.

Her current project combines her love of writing, tai chi, and life to help adults who suffer from chronic emotional pain. She believes that everyone has protective beliefs and behaviors that get in the way of living from the heart. Her upcoming book <u>A New Path to Healing: 81</u>

<u>Lessons from the Tao the Ching</u> is rich in contemplative teachings and practical solutions to help recognize and adjust daily habits. It taps into the wisdom of the body, so the unceasing mind chatter can rest. She guides her readers to release past wounds so they can transform into a simpler, more passionate and hopeful future.

Connect with Katie at <u>https://www.katiebrennanlifecoach.com</u>.

CHAPTER 12

Recreating Ourselves

by S. Kay McBreairty

The timing of this writing is apropos. In fact, I had a *final draft* ready for the editors when I had a new awakening. While I have recreated myself many times and have coached hundreds of people to do the same, here I am in the process of recreating myself again, due to several realizations over the last few days.

The time is now for me to get on with it – update my life mission statement and reconnect with my purpose. I realize I have become complacent. I believe in the obligation and have a desire to use my God-given talents to help others. My heartfelt mission is in service to helping children. I removed myself from several industries that didn't align with that mission: aviation, federal government, state government, law, and next technology.

Those are all good industries in which I gained knowledge, developed skills, learned to be responsible, and came to understand the high value I provide to those I serve. They just don't align with my purpose in this life.

Circumstances in my personal life taught me the need to develop self-esteem, in order to determine my purpose. I have always known I could do anything with God's help – I lacked not in confidence. But I erroneously felt unworthy to the point of feeling worthless. I worked on myself for many years. I read such books as *Self-love* by Robert Schuller, *Beyond Codependency* by Melody Beattie, and *Women Who Love too Much* by Robin Norwood, as well as going to Ala-non one night a week for ten years.

I was led to Ala-non during my marriage to a cocaine user in the eighties. Ala-non is an organization for the family members of alcoholics and other drugs. It was through that organization that I learned why I kept making unhealthy choices in life partners – choosing men that weren't capable of loving. One was a philanderer and another a substance abuser, for example. I came to learn how I had co-created chaos by needing to win over love that wasn't possible to be given. Feeling unworthy gets perpetuated until we learn to love ourselves.

Once I learned of these subconscious choices, I was able to raise my self-esteem. I was able to see that I deserve my heart's desires and success that align with my life's purpose. The steps I provide in aligning a "day job" to our purpose can also be used for aligning any of our choices to our purpose. For instance, I had a paradigm shift when I witnessed the way my parents looked at each other when I took Dad to see Mom in the nursing home. I dumped the guy I was seeing and would no longer settle for anything less than the kind of love I saw between those two people.

These are some of the reasons I became a life coach. While I don't coach children, I find that helping the parents, in turn, helps the children. Parents with self-esteem exhibit that and thus teach their children through their actions. And to exhibit our inherent worth, I wrote, produced, and starred in a seven-minute film that won an international film festival award (YouTube search: Mirror with Maverick Kay).

At the onset, when we choose to make a change, we don't have all the answers as to what the change will be or how things will work out. That can be the exciting part. Remember that the same physiological symptoms for fear are also some of the same for excitement: a pounding heart, sweating, hot or cold flashes, for instance; I choose excitement.

Take getting out of the military for example. When I chose to NOT be a *lifer*, there was a lot of unsolicited advice from those who were *stayin' in*. It went something like this: *What makes you think you can find work? Have you seen the unemployment rate? What will you do if it doesn't work out?* Not very supportive advice, but I found it exciting to be on an adventure.

As it turned out, I wasn't able to *stay in* in the end – I blew out my knee playing basketball for the Air Force and wasn't *worldwide qualified*. There went the career I didn't want – sure made the *getting out* decision easy. Life does us a good turn that way from time to time.

Don't get me wrong; the U.S. Air Force provided great value – serve my country, education, vocation, work experience, skill development… And years later I had a gig with Boeing as a contractor but left after less than a year. As you can see aviation just didn't align with my life mission even as great as planes are – consistently gets me to Europe from LA in ten hours flat.

Speaking of life doing us a good turn during times of uncertainty, take the pandemic. A serendipity of two years of people working outside of their vocation or being unemployed was the realization that they no longer wanted the vocation in which they had worked. In some ways, it would seem they woke up. It appeared as a breath of fresh air as they fantasized about what they might do next. One lady I met decided to buy a wine bar instead of going back to being an accountant.

Many other reasons may come into play for why you want to do something different: your kids are raised and through school so it's your turn, you're ready to write a new chapter of your life, you've gone as far as you care to in your current career, or you simply want to do something that feels more meaningful or perhaps be about leaving a legacy. Whatever the reason, these steps can apply.

Let's start with the step of reading and doing the exercises in *What Color is Your Parachute?* by Richard Nelson Bolles. While it is often referred to as a guide for job seekers, it helps with much more. One step is to determine what you like, why you like it, and what you're good at that you enjoy. Ok, that's more than one step, but all are in a similar category I call technical. This is crucial for getting clear as to how you see your skills and experience within other contexts and not by job titles. The book is an amazing guide, and most libraries have the current edition, as it is updated each year.

The book was my number one tool when I got out of the military. All that great skill building and work experience needed to be reworded into civilian speak. For instance, I had worked as a Legal Assistant in the Air Force. Well, that was a Paralegal at law firms when I got out. The duties between the two positions were the same – again just different nomenclature. Seems like a simple thing, but it truly was necessary. When I saw the glazed over eyes as I spoke of my experience, I tweaked my resume further to explain to civilians.

Once I managed the translation, I landed my first civilian job at a law firm in Seattle where one of the partners was a former governor. Then to a firm that sent me to their London office for two months, where I turned thirty. Best yet was the Attorney General's Office in the State of Washington (yes, the one that took down big tobacco).

Now let's talk non-technical, experiential steps. Getting out of our heads leads us to heartfelt, soul solutions – yes, the gut element. Here the real fun begins. Let's get into the mindset of openness, creativity, and receptivity.

Know that you are inherently worthy simply because you exist. Let's begin with some self-care. Why is focus on self-care important for our journey to recreate ourselves? I get a massage; I think, "That felt great, I'll do that again." Then I get a mani-pedi; I think, "I could get used to this." Then I get a facial; I realize, "I feel really good." Then I take a walk around the lake on the path under the trees; it dawns on me, "I deserve to feel this way." The self-worth / self-esteem boost puts us in a mindset of knowing we deserve and are worthy of our hearts' desires.

With this mindset, we can embark upon more experiential steps of finding and imagining what those desires are. Being a life coach when I lost my second parent, I did some of the same exercises I coached my clients when waking up from a life paradigm shift:

- Think back to what you wanted to be when you grew up – before you were old enough to talk yourself out of it. It is one of the few memories I have from my childhood; but remember it well, I do. I wanted to be an actress so I could say, "See, here I am." Yes, I am also an actress.

- Allow yourself to play within the context of having all the time and money you need to attain what you want, that neither are a limitation. Sometimes, we can enjoy our desires without an outlay of money. For instance, a friend of mine wanted to buy a yacht, which can be very expensive. What he came to realize was what he wanted was to enjoy a yacht. Next thing that happened was a friend of his had a yacht but needed to leave the area for a year. My friend got to use and care for that yacht for a year and got paid for it.

- With the foundation from these steps, now go to the next level of imagining your future knowing you can't fail – that once you take steps towards your goals, the Universe meets you more than halfway. *Success the Glenn Bland Method* by Glenn Bland helped me see my future with a balanced life in mind.

- Often our vision is full of material objects – the house, the sports car … That is all good, fun, and motivating. Even more so can be thought of the satisfaction that comes from our determining our next venture. For instance, my newest vision is waking up in the morning with joy knowing I get to help others full time to re-invent themselves and have their hearts' desires. Full time means no more **day job**.

- Now have fun defining your lifestyle. Lots of us start out with setting a goal to have a certain dollar amount in the bank – the million-dollar mark is common; I'll go ahead and raise my hand. But what I actually wanted was the lifestyle I believed that currency could afford me. For example, I didn't need that much for the first step of my vision – when a bill comes in, I pay it. I didn't want to worry about what day of the month it was and where it fell between pay days and what was due when. How freeing the shift has been.

I often say, "Change is good" – even the times that negative motivation has spurred me on to something else. That something else proved to be much greater than I could have even imagined. An example is the boss that I just couldn't work for any longer though the job was what I otherwise loved. It felt like a divorce – very painful. But once I started taking steps to change jobs and being open to the possibilities, an opportunity would surface that I hadn't even considered.

Allowing yourself to ponder and be open to what ideas surface on your journey can prove to be exciting and very rewarding. Here's to enjoying the process and the next chapter of your life.

S. Kay McBreairty

People often know only what they don't want and are in emotional pain from being stuck in that existence. They have all but given up and are close to being resigned to their less than desirable world.

As a professional coach and facilitator at McBreairty – Reaching Your Potential, Kay McBreairty has helped clients for over two decades find ways to bring joy into their lives – seeing that clients didn't have what they wanted because they didn't know what they wanted.

Believing everyone deserves to have their hearts' desires and has inherent worth simply because they exist, Kay focuses her coaching services on helping clients live those truths. First, clients use practices designed to help discover their hearts' desires, followed by visioning practices, goal setting, then the plan of action. Many people set goals just to become discouraged when they don't get results – not knowing goals are step three.

Client successes include finding joy in their current vocation, transitioning from the military to civilian life, and post-pandemic lifestyle changes. Kay's own journey began while in the U.S. Air Force with opportunities to retrain into different specialties – like retraining from an administrator to a paralegal.

Through the years, she has recreated herself several times. Each change brings more and more joy as each change more closely aligns with her life mission. An example of Kay's living a passion is when she wrote, produced, and starred in a film about her mid-life crisis. See it on YouTube at "Mirror with Maverick Kay."

Connect with Kay at www.reachingyourpotential.world.

CHAPTER 13

Being a Braver Woman

by Leanne C. Jones

The biggest source of unhappiness is boredom and stagnation. That static feeling of repetition and predictability, permeating every area of your life. Wake up, get up and do the same thing – on repeat. Our patterns become our prison that steal away our inspiration and interest. Whilst there is comfort in stability, it's also an illusion of safety that we can create, simply to feel safe in our existence. In 2020, I was turning forty. I asked myself, how was this happening? How had life gone by so quickly? As I pondered, there were another succession of ideas that I found difficult to tuck away and ignore. I continued to have these disruptive feelings of real growing inner discontent as I reflected upon my life up until this point.

My childhood was a deeply unhappy and uninspiring existence plagued with rigid discipline, a lack of creativity and conforming in ways to deflect Irish Catholic guilt. I experienced the horror of physical and emotional abuse and I was left homeless and penniless not long after revealing to my mother that I was a lesbian. My early adult years involved anxiety, depression, sofa surfing and working endless jobs to pay for my education.

My early twenties included limited finances, loneliness, moving around landing in places where I knew no one, family ostracization and a string of toxic failed relationships. It was like I was running away to escape myself, desperately seeking acceptance and love to try to develop some level of self-worth. I was different and I was acutely aware of my boyish appearance that highlighted that difference wherever I went. Because of this, I felt as if I had to work extra hard for outward acceptance so that I could feel safe and wanted. All I was doing all these years of my youth was indulging in complete self-sabotage.

I felt that I was never taken seriously because I wore the mask of the joker, the entertainer, to deflect from my differences, to be useful and worthy to others to make them like me. To somehow make up for the shame I felt about my background and my sexuality. To deflect to fit in and be respected for something at least, even if it was humour at my own expense to please others to feel safe and included. My life felt like an endless game of anxiety provoking snakes and ladders.

What I craved was stability, security, predictability, and peace for the first time in my life. I found this after twenty-one years in the Police service. The discipline forced me into developing structure in my life. This is not what drew me in, but it was something else much deeper.

Despite my background, I always had a yearning to be somebody who gives value to others as a human being, to connect and resonate with others and to help. The skill that I already possessed that made the job purposeful for me, was being able to resonate with human beings across the spectrums of life. From the homeless, to the wealthy, to those who felt broken, and this skill was borne from my own self-compassion and emotional acuity. When you are different and you are raised differently than others, when you experience isolation, hardship and failures, the gift you have is the development of high emotional intelligence. Being able to deeply connect and understand human behaviour from my own hypervigilance for gaining safety from not only being a survivor of childhood domestic abuse, but also as a gay woman. This difference served as a gift that allowed me to be able to quickly recognise behavioural cues, tone, and patterns in others, to communicate and really help the people I served.

I remember dealing with a verbal domestic situation aged thirty-one and literally assisting the family to resolve five years of miscommunication with both parties in the same room in under an hour, leaving the male and female completely speechless that they'd paid for years of couples therapy to cycle around the same patterns. My straight talking, yet sensitive, unapologetic, and direct approach with what I was sensing and observing seemed to be the conclusion that they needed.

That aha moment that drew the line underneath the sand for them. That experience never left me. "I can't believe you're just a cop, you're too good to be hidden behind that uniform, you could be helping thousands of people," he said to me as he thanked me. My colleague who nodded too, as he stood there quiet throughout, shifting on his feet and looking at the floor, not knowing what to say to them or where to start. This felt effortless to me.

What I didn't tell them was that this was a common reaction to my approach, throughout my career but also in my personal life, with friends and acquaintances that came to me for advice and help. I had served in three forces, including in London where after two decades, there weren't many things that phased me. I began to resonate deeply with what that man had said to me. Deep down, I knew he was right.

One of the things that I now say to all my clients in my practice is **"Don't just think it, know it."** There is an enormous difference between thinking or pondering over something and knowing it.

Knowing is really believing, knowing is certain, knowing is the powerful, solid truth that lies deep inside the veins of every one of us. The part that we can often ignore is remaining in our comfortable pattern prison. Those feelings can be disruptive, confusing, and scary, but do you know what's scarier? Having that inner knowing and passing up the opportunity to seek more about it. I often ask clients do you think you're not good enough? They tell me, yes. I then say to them, "Tell me, do you really know this to be true?" The answer is then, always a resounding, "NO."

That inner knowing is what propelled me to make a change with my life at age thirty-nine. To acknowledge my painful past as a gift, to start my company Braver Women®. I knew that I didn't want to simply retire from a stable career, draw my pension, pay off a mortgage and then grow old and simply die. I knew my life was worth so much more than what I was giving it credit for. I also knew my experiences counted for more than just pain and suffering. I know I was born for a reason and a purpose. We all are. Once we start listening to what we know about ourselves, rather than simply what we think. When you do this, you discover your possibilities for greatness by being brave enough to explore changes.

After seeing endless social media posts with coaches and therapists talking about personal change, I explored my own physical changes, emotional changes, and spiritual transformation. I wasn't joining the 5am club or drinking a ridiculous coloured smoothie and meditating for hours on end. My transformation was centred around listening to what I really knew about myself and my capabilities and giving myself the chance to find out, by taking action, making moves, and embracing changes toward my own development, no matter how scary it felt.

What I was becoming tired of watching was the disempowering messages delivered to millions on social media, encouraging a pop psychology culture of quick fixes and victimhood – helping people to remain comfortable within their discomfort, without making any changes to their circumstances. My approach was direct, and action based.

Wild horses won't change feelings, feelings change feelings and the only way to change your feelings, is to change your internal rules to give your subconscious a new perspective, a more balanced view of what you are capable of. Let me give you an example.

If you have the opinion about yourself that you are not good enough, the likelihood is that you'll have created a rule. A rule designed to cope within this problem feeling, a rule that you follow to ensure you aren't ever criticised, don't ever fail, are always liked and are seemingly in control. This is impossible to do all the time and the safety behaviours that follow by doing these rules are what's controlling you, meaning that you are stuck. Avoidance feels good in the short term, but it stops you from developing your confidence and self-esteem.

When we drop our safety rules and let them out of the pattern prison, we get new information to find out a more realistic and balanced view of ourselves, of what we are really capable of.

I was acutely aware of these rules when I wanted to coach and to become a therapist. The prospect of putting myself out there made me feel sick to the pit of my stomach with nerves. I'd spent my life in the confines of rules and regulations and breaking out to showcase myself and my teachings was daunting. I imagined all the homophobic comments that I would receive online, for my queer appearance not being the polished image of style and beauty.

Looking back, I now laugh that I even thought this way, it was old messaging that I'd bought into from my childhood, schooling, religion, social experiences, and discrimination that I had so frequently encountered. Here's the thing about discrimination, it's toxic hostility that's grounded in fear with irrational judgements, which are inherently unjust, based on pre-existing beliefs.

I had no idea who I was going to specialise in helping to begin with and whilst I was sitting on my surfboard bobbing up and down in the ocean one afternoon, when I was most relaxed in my mind, I asked myself three pivotal questions that gave me the answer to where I was going to break out and start to make a difference:

What was I passionate about?

What gave me purpose?

What was I proud about?

I was passionate about justice and fairness, my career in the police only served to highlight this more and more. What gave me an enormous amount of purpose was inspiring, teaching, and guiding others and it goes without saying, I have a tremendous amount of pride in who I am and all the parts of me that had shaped my identity and my life up to this point.

There must be thousands of other queer women out there in the world who feel the same way as I did, I thought, who are still struggling with rejection, coming out, isolation, loneliness, heartbreak, the not good enough fears, hiding their authenticity to fit in and feel safe, engrained rules keeping them trapped.

There was nothing that really existed in the world of personal development for queer women and I really questioned why this was. I needed this support when I was going through my own turmoil. I needed mentorship and guidance to be able to learn to thrive from someone who really understood what it was like to exist in the world feeling like a left-handed person, in a right-handed world. Something had to change in this world and the vision I had was bigger than I ever could have imagined.

Everything that I experienced up until this point in my life now started to add up, it made sense, it resonated and I was, for the first time grateful to have been through my own trauma, angst and despair because this difference. All this difference within me was now fuel for my own transformation. This inner knowing is what carried me forward, this inner knowing was more compelling and greater than the what ifs that were based on my old programming from the past. This is what I was supposed to be doing, my purpose had finally bloomed.

I now use my difference as my strength and draw upon everything I had learned, personally and professionally, to help LGBTQ+ women and awaken them to see that being different is not a disadvantage to keep them playing small. It's an opportunity to bring their unique perspectives and talents to the world, to live bravely as a braver woman, with more passion, purpose and pride.

Leanne C. Jones

Leanne C. Jones is a change work coach and therapist for LGBTQ+ women worldwide who are living with anxiety, low confidence and all the not good enough fears that hold them back from living to their true potential. Many women who have worked with her have experienced remarkable, life changing results. She is the founder of Braver Women® a bespoke therapy and coaching company, that specialises in solely working with LGBTQ+ women globally to live with more passion, purpose, and pride. Leanne passionately believes that change is possible for all LGBTQ+ women who have allowed the noise from outside of them, to determine how they think about themselves and show up in their lives. Many queer women are hugely inspired by her own personal story of bravery, where she took control of her life, by learning how to value her own self-worth. She now uses the adversities that she experienced as a huge vehicle for delivering her unique and precise coaching methods, teaching her clients exactly how to break problematic behavioural and thought patterns to gain a healthy perspective of themselves, so that they too, can experience a freer, happier, and more authentic life. She also helps her clients inspire other queer women around the globe, by sharing their stories of transformation after they have successfully worked with her. She is creating a movement of Braver Women worldwide.

Leanne loves spending her free time surfing the waves at home in Devon, UK and in nature with her beloved Patterdale Terrier, Bodhi.

Connect with Leanne in her Facebook group: LGBTQ+ Women's Emotional Empowerment | Anxiety Support- Braver Women®.

CHAPTER 14

The Moment That Forever Changed the Trajectory of My Life

by Lynda Sunshine West

I have never been a courageous person. I've never jumped out of a plane, hiked the Appalachian Trail, climbed Mt. Kilimanjaro, jumped from the Kármán line, or slept at the base of a volcano (yeah, I know people who have done all of those things). I've never had a desire to do anything like that. Riding rollercoasters is about as scary as I get.

In 2015, however, I decided to do something that a lot of people have never done. I broke through one fear a day for an entire year. Imagine yourself facing one fear a day… 365 days in… a… row.

The first question most people ask is, "Did you have a plan?" My response? "No, I didn't have a plan. If I were to call it a plan, it would look like this: every day, 365 days in a row before I get out of bed I am going to ask myself one simple question: 'What scares me?' I will lay in bed until the first fear pops into my head and my commitment to myself is to break through THAT fear THAT day." Yep, that was my plan. I didn't have a list of fears that I was going to break through. I had no idea if the fears were going to cost me a lot of money or if they were going to be free. I had no plan at all. All I knew was that I had a lot of fears that were stopping me from living my life and it was time I broke through them so I could change. And maybe my life would change. I had no idea what would be on the other side of that year, but I wanted something different.

That was the greatest year of my entire life. The growth that came from it was astronomical. Things I never even imagined would happen, happened. People I never would have imaged myself meeting, I met.

I remember it like it was yesterday. Sitting in traffic like I had done for 36 years. Driving to my 49th job working for a judge in the 9th Circuit Court of Appeals. Something was different that day, though. As the anger was permeating throughout my body, I started pounding my hands on the steering wheel and screaming, "Why am I here? What am I doing? I have no value. As a matter of fact, why is this planet here? There is no purpose to any of this. It doesn't make any sense." I continued my drive and finally arrived at work. As I trudged my way out of the parking lot and into the elevator, I was still feeling the pain of "WHY? WHAT? WHO?" I got into my office and started working.

The job I worked so hard to get (working for a judge in the Court of Appeals is the highest position I could work as a legal secretary) was wearing me down. It was eating the life out of me. I was living a groundhog day life, the same scenario day after day. Get up, eat breakfast, get ready for work, jump in the car, sit in traffic, go to work and punch the clock, eat lunch by myself, finish work, hop in the car, sit in traffic, get home, eat dinner with Wheatie (my husband), watch a little tv, go to sleep. Rinse and repeat five days a week. That was my life. The worst part is that I created that life. I worked really hard (sometimes 80 hours a week) to get ahead. It was freakin' hard.

When I got to work that day, those questions I asked while driving in traffic were answered. I got on Facebook and started scrolling around looking at my timeline and looking inside the different groups I belonged to at the time. There it was, the message I needed to hear at the exact moment I needed to hear it. It was from a woman named Liz. Her post was something like this, "I'm a life coach. I took some time off and I'm getting back into it. I'm looking for five women who want to change their lives."

I didn't know what a life coach was and how she would be able to help me, but I knew one thing, that I wanted to change my life. I was tired of the daily grind. I was tired of the daily traffic. I was tired of not knowing who I am. I was tired of being worthless. I was tired, tired and more tired.

I reached out to Liz and found out how she could help me and decided to hire her. That was the moment that forever changed the trajectory of my life. Hiring her took a lot of guts because I had never before paid that kind of money to work with somebody. It wasn't as much about paying for her services as it was about me believing that I deserved to spend that kind of money on myself. One thing I can tell you right now is that that was the greatest investment I ever made in myself; it is the greatest gift I have ever given to myself.

Don't get me wrong, I love my husband dearly, but sometimes we need to learn how to love ourselves so that we can love others more and greater. One of the many things that Liz did for me is teach me how to love myself. She saw something in me that I didn't see. And she kept after me to learn how to see it for myself.

"People come into your life for a reason, a season,
or a lifetime."
~Brian A. "Drew" Chalker

When I first heard the quote that people come into your life for a reason, a season, or a lifetime, I had no idea how real that was until I met Liz. She came into my life for a reason and a season. The reason was to help me to see that I do have value and that, while I was my own worst enemy, I could learn how to become my own best cheerleader. Liz helped me to see that there is a lot more about me that I have to offer this world that I needed to explore it to figure it out. Liz helped me to believe in myself. Liz helped me to embrace who I am and show up as that person.

Not every life coach is created equally. I was very fortunate to find Liz at exactly the time I needed her. She was perfect for me because she would press me to keep going. I completed every homework assignment. I was a good student. What I didn't realize at the time, though, was that it wasn't about being a good student as much as it was about becoming who I am meant to be. I wanted to get an A on the test. But there was no test.

I was 51 years old when I worked with Liz and it was the fastest five months of my life. As I was embarking on this journey of self-discovery, my life was shifting. Drastically. All for the better.

When our five months were up, I decided to continue on my own without Liz's help. There were so many things that she taught me during those five months that I was able to move forward without as much help.

January 1, 2015, when I woke up, I had an epiphany that fear was getting in my way and was stopping me from living my life. That was the day that I made the decision to break through one fear every single day for a year. That was the second greatest gift I had ever given to myself.

In this book, we're talking about midlife awakenings. If you decide to break through one fear a day for one week or even one month, you will see a huge shift in your life. It's a decision that can be made in an instant. I made my decision one fateful morning when I woke up.

What does a midlife awakening look like to you? How do you see yourself living the rest of your life? Do you want to do more and be more and have more? If so, stretch yourself out of your comfort zone and do something different today than you've ever done before. Make a decision that feels weird or reckless. You may be surprised with the results you get.

I started my midlife journey at age 51 and I have grown tremendously since that time. The last 50 years of my life will be the best 50 years of my life because I now, for the first time, know who I am and show up as that person on a regular basis. Had I not asked those questions that day that I was driving to work, I might still be living in the rat race wondering what I'm doing, why I'm doing it, and who I am here to serve. Fortunately, as human beings, we have the choice to make a difference in our own lives. We just have to choose and then do it.

What choices will you make? What changes will you make? What will the rest of your life look like? What action steps do you need to take in order to live the life you want to live?

Midlife doesn't mean we are dead. It is up to us to decide what we are going to do with the rest of our lives. I don't know about you, but I have chosen to live the rest of my life having as much fun as possible, hanging out with positive, uplifting, motivational people who are making a positive impact on the planet. That's how I plan on living the rest of my life. How do you plan on living yours?

Lynda Sunshine West

She ran away at 5 years old and was gone an entire week, came home riddled with fears and, in turn, became a people-pleaser. At age 51, she decided to break through one fear every day for a year and, in doing so, she gained an exorbitant amount of confidence to share her story. Her mission is to empower 5 million women and men to write their stories to make a greater impact on the planet. Lynda Sunshine West is the Founder and CEO of Action Takers Publishing, a Speaker, 23 Time #1 International Bestselling Author, Contributing Writer at Entrepreneur Magazine and Brainz Magazine, Executive Film Producer, and Red Carpet Interviewer.

Connect with Lynda Sunshine at

https://www.actiontakerspublishing.com.

CHAPTER 15

"Becoming"
Through the Sacred Art of Calligraphy

by Nahid Boustani

Part one - The sacred act:

Throughout history and in various cultures, of the many choices of creating art, calligraphy has been known as *sacred*. Many other forms of art could be approached as a mindful practice, yet none are considered *sacred*. To be sacred, one must connect to a higher level than the mind. They must receive messages from the soul/the spirit, thus good writing makes the truth stand out. I witnessed the sacredness of writing long before I read about it, so to approach it with reverence was natural as if getting ready for a date with the beloved. The one pen and the flow of ink would become a loving conversation. I read somewhere that calligraphers must work with the flow of energy if their work is to be alive which is not the same as being formally perfect. This is most overt in Taoism and Chinese calligraphy.

In my first class with a master calligrapher, which only went for one summer semester, I was asked how long I've been taking classes and with whom. The answer of course, was not any longer than a few minutes ago ... and the class is here. The teacher, of course, did not believe this until further questions didn't offer a better answer. I, however, could feel that I was in tune with the flow of life; enjoying picking up on something that's been my family's way[1], immersing myself in the aura of master calligraphers, and having my soul move my hand in smooth ways.

I was experiencing sacredness and learning to stay connected with it. I wasn't yet creating an art even though I was writing words beautifully. The mystics of the East receive the knowledge of the universe around them as songs and melodies. As a teenager, immersed in the soul of her geographic place, I was no different. There was an invisible dance going on in the

---

1 Both my father and mother, even though never practiced reed pen calligraphy, always cared for their handwriting.

universe, and it only needed me to become the vehicle to bring it onto paper. Calligraphy is frozen poetry, I read somewhere recently, and "I hear a melody," were the words given to me from a poet who admired my work.

It has come to crystallize for me, over the years, that we are here to be a creator and a co-creator. Both are crucial in the process of becoming our highest version. Creation is an inner expression, a yearning to show what we experience and be seen by it, just like the great Creator once did and to be a manifestation of Him/Her. Co-creating is to create in a way that's aligned with the greater movement of the universe. Like stars orbit in an orbiting galaxy.

In calligraphy, the work is created in one movement of the reed pen. Unlike painting, here, there is no second chance for changing what has landed on paper. All the intention, the thoughts, the feelings, and the energy is in that single concentrated movement. The line that's being stretched transfers to the substrate not only the artist's current state of being, but the whole process that brought the artist to that state; the creative energy exists in the journey to creation rather than in the act of creation. Connect what's been in history and what's taking place in the present to a higher purpose that's been transmitted from the universe, and the calligrapher is reflecting the intention of the cosmos, manifesting for a co-created future.

As I dive deeper into my artistic identity, I take frequent stops to break through my shadows and rearrange myself into a more authentic place. Huh! A moment of surprise as I listen to my own words. They are not mere cliches. This is true that I am becoming through my practice. Receiving takes trust and trust requires authenticity. You can't trust what is poured through the heart of the universe if you're not authentically there to experience it. For authenticity is the ultimate integration of intentionality and wisdom; the alignment of values/ virtues, emotions, and behaviors, so the light that's being poured flows through unanimously.

Among the most critical re-arrangements were the *rules*. I learned that rules of any kind, whether existing within the artist, the genre of work, or the culture are limitations. What are considered as guiding principles must give their place to assumptions that are set by the artist for the sake of the short- or long-term results. Let's explain this further. For creation to happen, the artist must break or at least bend *rules* as rules direct us to average behaviors, so that we fit in. If we are ever going to create something that's exceptional, average is nothing to aspire to. Instead of sounding like others, we must hear the unique calling within us, nourish it, and cherish it, so it blossoms into something extraordinary.

Traditional calligraphy is founded on strict rules for shapes, angles, and arrangements. Most calligraphers introduce themselves as the follower of a master. They earn their credibility by the fame of the master. How was I to be considered a calligrapher if I never had a Master? Many made me feel that I still needed to earn the right to existence. My mind would always argue, how was I going to create a piece of art if I followed strict rules? I observed that often the most creative ideas come from those who've mastered the rules to such a degree that they can see past them or from those who never learned them at all. I was among the latter with the exertion to unlearn the little I had learned, so I could hear and honor my own true voice.

Could I hear my own voice? Perhaps I was always hearing, but could I listen so that I could honor? Listening requires suspending disbelief, allowing, and receiving without preconception and judgment. The result is a collection of perspectives which are all correct and all contribute to the greater understanding of what's being transmitted. Could I hold all these perspectives and still make my own mark, make an artwork? With allowing, perspectives gave their place to space, a place of unity, of knowing, and that was the stamp of approval on everything I made. There, in the presence of that space, whatever I did became an artwork.

Sounds magical? It is and it is not if only we know that's indeed truth, and in truth, flaws are flawless because truth speaks for itself.

Part two - Reminiscence:

Down the memory lane, while I was recovering from postpartum blues, revelations poured in, and I made a pledge to catch them for future comers. The universe was speaking, and I was honored to be the chosen one. It impregnated me with a knowing and pictured it for me with a *dot* and a *circle*; the seed that grew to become the backbone of my *becoming* movement.[2]

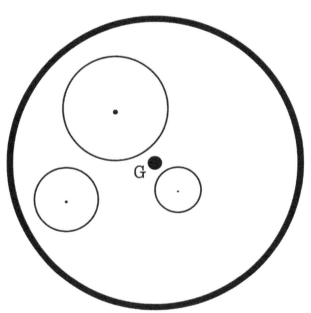

---

2 "Be the dot, Be the presence," is a social practice art and a movement inviting everyone to nurture the relationship between the local self and the infinite self for receiving creativity. And to merge the centered selves for an experience of unity within humanity at G.

Who are we? We are the drops in an ocean; we all must have heard, but the answer was coming to me this time in a more quantum manner, without any elements and only through a subtle and invisible yet powerful knowing; an acknowledgment of consciousness and attention. Who I was depended upon my awareness. The drop in the ocean could indeed be the ocean if it could see itself. I was the *circle* of infinity when my attention was extended, and I was a *dot* in the circle when my attention was focused there. The more centered this dot became (in itself and inside the circle), the better it could touch the circumference of infinity. Thus, started my journey of quiet to be the dot and be the presence that extended to an infinite edge.

Expressions became my solace … art, writing, and recreating the heritage of my homeland, with calligraphy as my main tool for depicting the bi-locational state of my psyche, stretching from West to East. There were songs in the quiet, jewels in the presence, and glory in the space!

Like a dreamcatcher, I would catch them and let my hands transfer them onto paper. Life was no longer a mere series of tasks, encounters, and goals to chase. It was participation in the dance, choreographed by the great creator, and riding on the joy of being a vessel for the greater truth. I never knew that which was being planted would grow into a social platform and a community for others to join. All I wanted was to quench the thirst for expression and I little understood this is indeed why we are on this Earth; to be the vessel.

To be in order to become … It was only through being and surrendering that I could allow expressions to flow and, simultaneously, see the potential for becoming the next version of myself. Grace was pouring and the force of gratitude and unconditional love was changing my perspective of where I was standing. Right at the surface water of a half-full, half-empty glass, beneath me was all that I had, and above me all the unrealized potentials, I again had. From that perspective, the level of the water didn't matter; it didn't matter if I was standing at point one or two. It was not even a glass; it was an infinite world. Normal scale and comparisons dissolved, and I had access to all.

●
●
●
●
●
●
●
●
●
●
● 1
●

2

There was a merging of grace and the laws of physics. There was an awakening to purpose, possibilities, humanity, and unity. There was an awakening to the power of surrendering and observing. There was an awakening to a calling, a calling to lead spaces with spirituality and creativity. The pulsation of life in stillness and the abundance of love in presence, was not to be dismissed. It was to be trusted and manifested.

AIA ... Attention, Intention, Acknowledgement; the triangle of the quiet conversation for embodying the truth of time and space. In a hologram of infinite blessings, I was asked to reveal my deepest desire, my intention, so love would direct into a solidified place. "What do you want to do with your life?" It was a question of the universe for me.

"I want to serve and lead by serving," was my answer. As I held the intention dear, my attention stayed with the beloved. An aha moment, a soft nudge, an unexpected call, a clear knowing, a sudden urge, and I would acknowledge them all with a silent nod. There, in stillness, I forged ahead. There, in yielding, I delivered the truth. There, in presence, creative sparks tingled in the air. My creation was not just an expression of myself, but an answer to someone else's quest, a solution to another's chaos, a seed of change to a place in need; a thermos of many dimensions and manifestations.

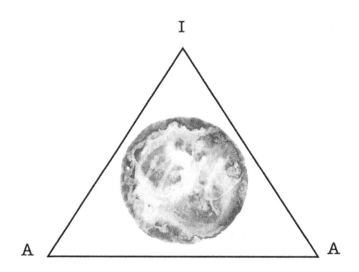

Part three - The artist:

I have an innate reverence for teachers and a love for learning. Growing up, I was notorious for being a great student, both academically and morally. A natural wise owl, I later explored the role of the teacher. I was great at speaking in others' languages and traveling up and down the complexity spectrum to explain almost any subject. I learned that real teaching would bring in an insight beyond the subject in hand. Real teaching would make a change in the system of thinking, unlocking possibilities, and equipping another with processing means in order to understand. That was transitioning to the role of a coach. Becoming an artist was taking the learning, the doing, the knowing to yet another level.

The artist's identity, contrary to the common belief, is beyond the persona created around the work. The creator is the ultimate identity, and for me, the avant-garde practice of a strictly structured art form was my soul's calling for claiming its artistic identity; a spiritual authority for self-actualization founded on virtues and allowing. My artistic identity precedes all else, walking ahead of me in life, wanting to serve by co-creating, paving the way, and inviting the rest of me to participate. Like a fairy waving the magic wand and setting me on a path to hold the torch for igniting creativity for the highest good of all.

Nahid Boustani

Nahid Boustani is an Iranian American self-proclaimed artist who contributes her art to the arduous practice of staying in presence. Growing up in the East side of the planet, she is deeply connected with the ancient poets, philosophers, and mystics of the region; and Persian Calligraphy as her family heritage and her main tool to share the spirit of art. On her platform Hozur, she aims to provide opportunities for others to acknowledge their innate creator.

As a data scientist, she sees through the double lenses of being anthropocentric and data savvy. In her corporate life, she is passionate about leading by harnessing the highest potential of individuals, and through holding a space for discovering creative solutions. Studying in multiple fields of engineering in both the US and her home country, she yearns to utilize her system thinking and her knowledge of data for impacting lives and saving environments.

Mother of 13- and 11-year-old boys, she considers her family, home, and garden to be her grounding plane. The earthly bonding that they offer is where she takes refuge when she needs a long patient pause between her endeavors.

Connect with Nahid at https://linktr.ee/nahidtr

CHAPTER 16

Words and Colors

by Sally Green

I'll never forget the day I turned 50. It was pretty much like any other day - I went to work that morning and stopped by the grocery store on my way home. While I was shopping, my phone rang—it was my husband. He had shocking news. He said there had been a shooting at an elementary school in the next town. It was December 14th, 2012. As I reached the checkout, I overheard the cashier talking about it too. I got in my car and turned on the radio to hear more. When I got home, I turned on the local news and found out that a person with a gun had gone into a school in Sandy Hook, Connecticut, and shot some teachers and students.

Later that day, I received a phone call from someone at my church. They thought that one of my former Sunday school students, Vicki Soto, might have been one of the victims. Vicki and her family were involved in our church, and it was devastating to think she might be gone. I prayed and hoped it wasn't true. Sadly, it was. It was an incredibly sad day for so many people in Connecticut, as we mourned the loss of young children and teachers. It was hard to imagine how the families affected by this tragedy could ever find the strength to overcome such a terrible event.

I attended the memorial service for Vicki. It was a day filled with lots of tears, hugs, and memories of a beautiful young woman, who was taken from us too soon.

The Sandy Hook Elementary School shooting shook my world. It made me realize just how fragile and unpredictable life can be. Amid all the sadness, I was amazed by the bravery and resilience of the people in my community. At that time, our church didn't have a pastor, and I was helping out in the office. I couldn't believe the number of calls we received from people offering prayers and donations to support the affected families. It showed me that there is still kindness and goodness in the world.

After the tragedy, I started thinking about my own life and the things that really mattered. The everyday routine I had felt was suffocating, and I needed a way to deal with all the emotions I was feeling inside.

One evening, some friends invited me to a fun event at a local art studio for a Paint-n-Sip acrylic painting class. It was there that I felt a spark of inspiration and a strong desire to reconnect with my artistic side. I felt ready to begin a journey of self-discovery through art. So I started by taking basic painting classes online and learning all about different painting mediums, such as acrylics, watercolors, and mixed media art.

This artistic journey I embarked on has opened up a whole new world for me. It's not just about painting pictures—it's about expressing my emotions in ways that words can't capture. Through art, I've learned to dig deep into my feelings and understand myself better. I've found that art helps me reflect on who I am and lets me grow as a person. Each step I take on this amazing journey teaches me something new, helping me become the best version of myself.

As I continued exploring my creativity, I discovered another passion inside me—writing. Words became my shield and sanctuary. I poured my heart out onto paper, creating poems that helped me heal and gave me an outlet to let go of some of the pain I was carrying.

Art and writing became powerful tools for me to cope with the tragedy at Sandy Hook Elementary School. I want people to know that even in the darkest times, there's still beauty and hope to be found. That's why I want to share my journey, especially for those who might be going through tough times or feeling lost.

After the Sandy Hook tragedy, I recognized that life could change in an instant. It made me think about what truly matters—love, compassion, and the connections we have with others. It made me want to make a difference and use my creativity to spread positivity and hope.

You see, art and writing have this amazing ability to bring people together. They can help us understand each other's experiences, share our feelings, and find comfort in knowing that we're not alone. Through my art, I've been able to create beautiful images that capture emotions and tell stories. Through my writing, I've been able to express my thoughts and feelings in a way that resonates with others.

My journey is not just about creating art and writing for myself. It's about reaching out to others who might need a little spark of hope or a reminder that they are not alone.

Embracing my creative side was a blessing. I developed a passion for painting and started hosting and teaching paint classes for family and friends. Soon after, I reached out to senior centers and began leading classes. By the fall of 2019, I chose to pursue this path further and I began creating a business plan.

I intended to start full force in January 2020. I organized monthly Saturday morning Coffee and Canvas art classes at my church, along with Friday night Paint-n-Sips. Promoting my services as a mobile painting class for women, I had several sessions booked into the first quarter of 2020 and a major fundraiser scheduled for the beginning of April. Then at the end of February, we went into lockdown and all my classes were canceled. I was devastated, but I wasn't defeated.

So, here's the thing—I love writing and painting, but when it comes to being organized, I'm not exactly the best. You see, I had this collection of poetry that I had been writing for over eight years, and it was all over the place. I had poems in my car, on my phone, on my computer, on random bits of paper, and tucked inside notebooks. It was a total mess!

I had this idea, to turn my collection of poetry into an eBook. It seemed like the perfect way to share my poetry with others, especially during a time when we were all craving connection and inspiration. So, I rolled up my sleeves, dusted off my computer skills, and got to work.

Now, let me tell you, it wasn't an easy task. I had to gather all those scattered pieces of poetry and bring them into one place. It was like a treasure hunt, searching through my car, digging into my phone's notes, scrolling through my computer files, and flipping through countless pages of notebooks. But little by little, I found them all and started to see the bigger picture.

As I sat there, surrounded by stacks of paper and digital files, I couldn't help but feel a sense of accomplishment. It was like piecing together a puzzle, each poem fitting perfectly into the whole. After much sorting, organizing, and tweaking, I finally had my collection—a beautiful blend of words and emotions that I had poured my heart into.

Formatting the eBook was a whole new adventure. It was like creating a mini-masterpiece, carefully arranging each page to evoke the emotions I wanted to convey.

When I hit that magical *publish* button, I felt a mix of excitement and nerves. I was so afraid of what people would say, I didn't tell anyone about publishing my poetry book. I thought people would randomly find it, but they did not. I never sold a single copy.

At the time I published my poetry book, something super exciting happened—I was given the chance to contribute a chapter to a collaboration book! You can bet I jumped at that opportunity faster than a cheetah chasing its prey. And let me tell you, that experience changed everything for me.

Being part of that multi-author book introduced me to a whole new world of connections and friendships. I met some truly incredible people. But here's the cool part—being in a book didn't just make me feel like a superstar author (even though that was pretty awesome), it also opened doors I never even knew existed. It was like discovering a secret passage to a whole realm of opportunities in the world of anthologies and book publishing.

Being part of that collaboration book taught me the importance of seizing opportunities and stepping out of my comfort zone. It showed me that sometimes, the biggest rewards come from taking risks and being open to new experiences. It's like when you dare to ride that roller coaster for the first time, feeling a mix of excitement and nervousness, but ultimately knowing that the thrill is worth it.

Let me tell you, being part of these collaboration books has been a wild ride. It has pushed me to explore different writing styles, collaborate with others on creative projects, and challenge myself to express ideas in fresh and exciting ways.

Tapping into your creativity is not just for artists or writers. It's for everyone. Whether it's painting, writing, singing, dancing, or any other form of self-expression, it's about finding what brings you joy and using it to make a positive impact on the world around you.

Sometimes life throws us curveballs, and it's okay to feel lost or overwhelmed. Remember that you have the power to turn those challenges into opportunities for growth. Embrace your creativity, explore new passions, and never be afraid to share your unique voice with the world. Your experiences, your stories, and your perspective matter.

As I look back on my journey of self-discovery through art and writing, I am grateful for the healing it has brought me and the connections I have made along the way. It has shown me that even in the face of tragedy, there is resilience, strength, and beauty to be found.

Don't be afraid to tap into your creative potential. Let your imagination soar, express yourself freely, and let your unique voice be heard. Use art and writing as tools to navigate life's challenges, celebrate its joys, and make a positive impact on those around you.

The tragedy at Sandy Hook Elementary School was like a storm that tore through our lives, leaving devastation and heartbreak in its wake. It shattered our community to its very core, and it felt like the world had been turned upside down. But amid this darkness, something incredible happened—we found strength in unity, resilience in the face of despair, and a glimmer of hope to guide us through.

Through art, I discovered a way to breathe life back into my spirit. With every brushstroke and splash of color, I found a glimmer of beauty and a sense of peace. It was like a form of therapy, allowing me to pour my emotions onto the canvas and create something that spoke volumes, without uttering a single word. Through each stroke, I found strength and resilience.

Writing poetry became my sanctuary, a refuge where I could pour out my thoughts and feelings onto the page. It was a way to make sense of the senseless, to find meaning in the midst of tragedy. With every word I penned, I felt a weight being lifted off my shoulders, as if the act of writing itself had the power to heal wounds and mend broken hearts.

This journey of resilience and hope is far from over. It's a road that continues to unfold before me, leading me to new revelations and unexplored territories of self-discovery. Through art and writing, I have unearthed parts of myself that I didn't know existed—the strength to persevere, the courage to face adversity, and the resilience to find light in the darkest of times.

In the aftermath of tragedy, I have learned that healing is not a destination, but a lifelong process. It's a journey we undertake together, hand in hand, supporting one another as we navigate the complexities of grief and the pursuit of hope. Through art and writing, I have found a community of like-minded people who understand the power of creativity in healing wounds and rebuilding lives.

Remember, you are not alone on this journey. We're all in it together, supporting and uplifting one another. So, embrace your creativity, share your stories, and spread love and understanding in the world. Who knows? Maybe one day, you'll inspire others with your own incredible journey of self-discovery through art and writing.

Sally Green

Sally Green is the Vice President of Author Development at Action Takers Publishing. She works with writers to help them develop their stories and become bestselling authors. Action Takers Publishing specializes in themed multi-author collaboration books in which each person writes a chapter and becomes part of a community of like-minded authors. In addition to collaboration books, they also publish solo books.

At the age of 58, Sally realized that she was really good at taking care of everyone else, but really bad at taking care of herself. So, she embarked on a journey of self-care that began with investing in herself and contributing to a multi-author book. Sally is an inspirational speaker, a multiple times International Bestselling Author and is in the process of writing her own book titled: The Self-Care Rockstar due to launch in 2023.

In her spare time, Sally enjoys painting and teaching acrylic paint classes to local senior centers, Women's groups, and Children's summer camps.

Connect with Sally at https://www.actiontakerspublishing.com/.

CHAPTER 17

A Deafening Internal Echo Chamber

by Samantha "Dr. Sam" Graber

Allow me to paint the scene for you.

In it, there sits a woman. She could be anyone you know.

To the outer world, she is strong and centered. She is the one everyone else turns to in times of trouble.

All the while, she sits at rock bottom. Where she slips silently into a deafening internal echo chamber. Steeped in red wine. Alone with her thoughts. Unable to escape.

You'd never know it from looking at her, there. Where she sits.

That woman was me in 2017.

Those thoughts were dark yet telling of an awakening to come. Back then, I had no clue what they were trying to tell me.

I'd never sat with my thoughts before. Truth be told, I wanted to do anything but sit with these thoughts. They were not kind, nor were they helpful. At least, not until I fine-tuned my listening skills and started speaking their language.

Ripping Me Apart at the Seams

At that point in time, my inner thoughts were ruthless. Bent upon ripping me apart at the seams. It was as if they were trying to expose everything I'd hidden from myself (and everyone else) over a lifetime.

Though it almost broke me, this reconciliation was something I desperately needed.

You see, I'd always been moving. I never sat with my thoughts.

Sure, I'd go to a yoga class here and there. True to form, I'd rush through them, half of my mind set on doing it right and the other half ticking away at my to-do list for after class.

When I was in motion, doing all the things I had no time to self-examine. Much like the people I now serve, I was existing to serve others at the expense of myself.

Marinating in Shame

There comes a point in every woman's life when her body mounts a mutiny. Her mind rides shotgun and appears to be reading a map of Mars turned upside down.

All in all, it is a tumultuous time and a downright confusing one as well. Not to mention, it's lonely. This time in life can be so very lonely.

That was what I was experiencing back in 2017. Remember, I was doing it in the closet. Marinating in shame, because I should power through it like I did every other thing in my life. Just like a modern, independent Wonder Woman.

Growing up, I idolized Lynda Carter. So, it's no wonder (pun not intended) that I stepped forth and channeled her in everything I did.

To add to my should-fest, I am a seasoned holistic doc with then twenty-five years of direct patient care under my belt, though expanding at that time. I was completely blindsided by what was happening to my own body and brain right around the forty-five-year marker.

Turns out I was in perimenopause.

I was intellectually prepared for and actually looking forward to menopause, mind you. I had no desire to get pregnant again, in fact it was a worry and totally tanked my libido even prior to perimenopause. I couldn't wait to no longer be fertile, so I was welcoming menopause with open arms.

But, and it's a big but, I had no idea that along with the changes in my period, I'd experience a flood of trauma residue (unresolved trauma) that would all but take me out of the game. I can't say I was suicidal, but I didn't want to stay alive. That felt like too much.

Just as I'd almost let go, I'd find strength returning to my grip. That back-and-forth went on for a few years.

Peri Pushes Back

You see, there is no powering through perimenopause. In fact, in my experience, the more we try to power through, the more peri pushes back. Hard. She finds all the cracks in the fabricated facade and merci-lessly exploits them. For our own good in the long run, it turns out. But in the thick of it, she's one helluva b!tch to go toe-to-toe with.

During one of my spiritual pleadings, early on in this transition, I vowed that I would not let another woman suffer through perimenopause like I was. If I just made it through it!

Ever pray to the porcelain gods?

It was like that, but the nauseating head-spinning feeling did not end in twenty-four hours or less. I was having a very difficult go at it and looking back, I'm not sure how I held on in the beginning.

As of this moment, I'm still in the throes of peri, but I am no longer going it alone. You don't have to either. No matter where along the hormonal continuum you find yourself today, if you jive with my vibe, I invite you to look into the community of midlife women I'm cultivating around me. (Check my bio for details.)

Humbled and Inspired

Midlife is fluid in timing, and I see it as that time in which we have some life experiences that have both humbled, as well as inspired us. We know there is so much more we want to explore, so we're willing to rally and set forth on a path that actually serves us.

It is at this point in life that we know certain things or circumstances need to change, but as I humbly share herein, even those of us who serve others in their healing need an outside assist.

A seasoned perspective from those who've been there, done that compresses the learning curve in life. It also helps us proactively prepare for what is yet to (possibly) come.

What Does That Say?

A business coach once said to me, "You can't read the label from inside the jar." That has stuck with me for years. I say it to others on a regular basis, in fact.

In a nutshell, it means that we can't see what's transpiring when we're in the thick of it (in the jar). From relationships, to business, to perimenopause, when we're smack dab in the middle of it, it is challenging to gain perspective (read the label).

The jar, also referred to as the box, is our ego. That part of us that came about in response to anger, shame, or fear as a child. Something happened to us and our, let's say 5-year-old selves, made a decision about others and the world-at-large in response. A decision that served us then (we survived) but, most likely, sabotages us now.

We all do it, but it's something we don't talk about. Like so many things that actually matter in life.

We have never been taught how to take inventory of past experiences and the emotional residue left behind (unresolved trauma). We carry that stuff with us everywhere we go. The term baggage is so spot on!

Prior to doing my own inner work, which is a continual work in progress, I was lugging around a full set of Samsonites. I've got a carry-on and a backpack now. Much progress has been made, and more is yet to come.

I study Dr. Joe Dispenza's work intensively. As he so succinctly states, "Most people try to create a new personal reality as the same personality, and it is impossible."

He further elaborates that if we want to create a new personal reality, then we have to start thinking about what we've been thinking about and change our inner narrative.

Journey to My Whole-Self

Enter the Enneagram. I was originally introduced to this piece of ancient wisdom some twenty-plus years ago, but I lumped it in with all the other personality typing shenanigans and dismissed it. I was in no way ready to embrace its wisdom. Had I known then what I know now, my life would have been radically different. As would the lives of my children.

It's for them that I rolled up my sleeves and started the work. It's for me that I continue doing it today.

Until I shifted my mindset and approached the Enneagram as a tool to help me better understand what makes me tick and what makes me a ticking time bomb, my wounded child (my ego) was at the wheel.

As I shifted in healing, so much unfolded for me. It was as if the Divine Feminine said gently, "Let go, I've got you."

Something I so desperately needed to hear.

I'd been rejected and dismissed by those who are supposed to love me. Both my parents, at different life stages, turned their backs on me. One as a child and one when I was pregnant with my third daughter.

Those experiences had a profound and lasting effect that crippled me emotionally and sabotaged my every relationship.

Making My Healing My Highest Priority

When we are more holistically congruent, in our thoughts, in our behaviors, and in our intent, all we bring to the world is congruent as well. I can honestly say, I had the best intentions in all I did.

I have always wanted to help people heal from their hurt. I understand myself and my past so well now that I deeply comprehend why that desire has charted the entire course of my life.

The first half of my career as a holistic chiropractor focused on the physical aspect of people's pain. I assisted thousands over the years, but often found that for some, the emotional pain could override what was no longer physically present.

That always stumped me. How some could look and perform physical tests perfectly, but still have crippling pain. Through my own healing, I now comprehend better the connection between body and mind. It is why I focus my work where I do now, at the intersection of the head, the heart, and the body.

Aligning Our Head, Heart, And Body

Pairing my newly gained perimenopause perspective with decades of experience in the holistic healing field led to a discovery I call the KNOW | FEEL | DO Methodology. It is how we align our heads, our hearts, and our bodies.

In a nutshell, the KNOW | FEEL | DO Methodology is a framework that helps you unravel your experiences, shed that which no longer serves you, lean into what does, and pursue the missing pieces of your personal development puzzle.

It takes the form of a trio of circles that when overlapped, as in a Venn diagram, form an area in which you can home in to then get to work.

The KNOW portion of the methodology has to do with the intelligence that resides in our heads. The thinking, the knowing, the understanding of it all; that type of intelligence.

The FEEL portion of the methodology has to do with the intelligence residing in our hearts. The feeling, the emoting, the empathizing; those are some of the qualities we house in our hearts.

The third part of our trio is the DO portion. This is the type of intelligence that resides in our bodies, in our gut, at our core. It's the intelligence we feel deep within. We just know it to be true.

There's Power in Community

I love to learn new things. Consider me a perpetual student of life.

All too often I would study and yet still fall short on application. This was especially true when it came to my personal development journey. I'm a perfectionist-in-recovery, but back in 2017 and 2018, that aspect of me ran amuck.

Remember the spiritual pleadings I mentioned earlier? I made good on my promise by bringing the Unraveling Together Community to life.

The Unraveling Together Community is where women connect and pursue a more holistic approach to their changing bodies and minds with a focus on their midlife metabolism and menopause, from pre- to peri- to post-. Through masterclasses and co-working sessions, we cultivate more meaning in our individual lives while tapping into the collective wisdom of women.

Samantha "Dr. Sam" Graber

Samantha "Dr. Sam" Graber is an author, podcast host, keynote speaker and Holistic Transformation Coach for women ready to stop sacrificing their health in their pursuit of success.

After a multi-decade career as a holistic chiropractor, she orchestrated her own transformation from burnt out doc to impassioned community curator.

The Unraveling Together Community is where women connect and pursue a more holistic approach to their changing bodies and minds with a focus on their midlife metabolism and menopause, from pre- to peri- to post-. Through masterclasses and co-working sessions, they cultivate more meaning in their individual lives while tapping into the collective wisdom of women.

Connect with Dr. Sam at https://drsamgraber.com.

CHAPTER 18

Live Your Best Life!

by Simone Bosman

I started asking myself, "Is this it? This can't be it. I must be meant for more than being a work 'slave' for the wealthy and successful. If this is supposed to be 'it,' I don't want it. I don't want to live to work, but work to live and enjoy it without sorrow and with happiness."

This was March 2020, when the first lockdown started in Germany. It was all over the news that employees were now getting only 60 percent of their wages. Right then, I decided I did not ever want to depend on just one resource for my finances and on employers and governments. Not ever!

I also had this deep sense of feeling that I *do* have the power to take my own life in my hands, to be the director of my own movie called life.

Up to that moment, I was very good at sabotaging every great idea I had, and I didn't know why. I also couldn't remember a single moment in life without financial worries!

In my early childhood, my Dutch father worked full time, and my German mother was a stay-at-home mom, spending all the money on excessive amounts of stuff that happened to be on sale and nice things for herself. She was not a loving mother, and it was evident that her children were in the way.

My younger brother and I, as well as our little dog, experienced a lot of physical abuse from our mother. Because of this abuse, my little brother and I took our dog to an animal shelter, because at least we could protect him this way. Imagine a four- and six-year-old bringing a dog to a shelter. They didn't accept him, because when they asked, "Do your parents know?" our answer was "No." So, we tied him to a tree in front of the shelter, hoping someone would take him.

Our parents fought a lot with each other, both physically and screaming. We were out on the streets a lot, playing or just to not be at home. Because there, we could do nothing wrong. In the end, a kindergarten teacher discovered the bruises on my little brother, and our new life started. Our parents divorced, and we were then raised by my father and his family—the happiest part of my childhood. Our father remarried, and the new "mom" really did her best but probably never realized how damaged her two new children were.

By that time, I just had two years of bullying and daily beating in primary school behind me. I ended that period myself when something snapped, and I raged for maybe five minutes on the boy who cut off my hair in the middle of a test. He had two facial bones broken. After that, no one tried anything on me anymore.

For a long time, I felt proud. Because of that, no one bothered me anymore physically. Then, rather than being bullied, I became invisible. For me, that was not necessarily bad, because not being noticed is not being hurt, even though it was very lonely.

As I met my husband at the age of twenty-one, it was the first time in life where I felt really, completely loved and accepted the way I am. He truly is "my better half." Together, we have struggled with finances up until the pandemic started, but also with standing up for us toward other people outside the two of us. We have been together now for twenty-seven years.

Besides the pandemic, two major events happened to us that led to my awakening in March of 2020.

The first one: In 2010, we moved to Germany to start our own hotel. We, unfortunately, were betrayed by a Dutch man who owned the hotel and rented it to us. Four months later, we were thrown out, with our two children, ages five and seven. That was the sixteenth of December 2010. I remember it so vividly because there was a LOT of snow! The man said he was going bankrupt, and he needed us gone. Apparently, we had a bad contract, so there was nothing we could do but save ourselves. Our kids suffered greatly from that event. We also lost our home and a lot of money.

The second one: The Dutch government handled a case of fraud of foreign people working in the Netherlands very bad over twelve years of time and, as a result of that, many people had to quickly pay back a lot of child support-tax money. It could be because of little mistakes made by either the government or the citizen. We still don't know what the case was with us.

This all began before our hotel adventure. We decided to register as possible victims, and after a couple of years, we finally were acknowledged as victims and got a bit of money back. But trusting government people is not that easy anymore.

Both events really swept us off our feet, but working hard on our debt and getting money back from the government has helped us pick back up again.

And then the pandemic started. No one could work, and we got only sixty percent of our salary. This might be very good compared to a lot of other countries, but our expenses were high. We were still paying off debts because of our hotel adventure and the child support-tax drama, we had to pay rent, buy food, and we had everyday expenses to live. It was a struggle. It made me angry, and I decided to learn as much as possible to never let that happen again.

There was this Dutch company that organized a lot of free webinars about growing in life, personal development, finances explaining, etc. I watched them all, and since I heard them mention Tony Robbins, I figured I might study him and joined his free 5-day challenge. This was such an eye opener for me. I learned that I was under the impression of not being and feeling good enough. I finally discovered how I never came to execute my great ideas and why I always seem to have bad luck! I had been living like that for forty years and was programmed or set up to live like this from the start. No wonder I could not get ahead in life!

I did not want the short time left to be spent the same. So I had to rewrite my story, and I did. This whole period became a catalyst, starting with the acknowledgement of the Dutch government. Since then, I have learned a lot about self-development and getting over trauma, and I have been studying Tony Robbins, and discovered Bob Proctor along the way and studied him as well.

So, you can say, the moment I decided to take my life into my own hands, things started to change for me, in a good way. Because of opening up to the possibility that good things are meant for me too, I started appreciating more what I have, and I met the most wonderful people (like co-author Ewa), and I have already reached half of my vision board. Also, things are changing very good financially. The whole period of studying was a lot to discover on me, and at times, it made me slip back to anxiety. The key to the anxiety, for me, was moving and taking care of my body. Of course, our wonderful chow-chow dog Luke helps me with that too.

The "I am not good enough" Simone still pops up in my head every now and then, but I now know how to tell it to shut up. A little motivation video of "Team Fearless" did a great job in helping me with that. It gave me my new daily mantra, which is: I am capable, I am powerful, I do have the power, I am blessed, I am destined for great things!! My time is coming, I am ready, I am willing, I have everything I need to succeed, and I am ready to earn my results!

Before this period, I didn't understand why the road to success is more important than the actual goal of success. I got this beautiful poster from my yoga teacher that has the following quote: If you reach the top, keep climbing. And I also didn't get that before. This awakening brought me a renewed sense of purpose and meaning, and a greater appreciation for life.

While studying, I discovered that, for me, it was all about self-image. Everything starts with that. I got a little bit of extra help with that through a hypnosis session and more through timeline therapy.

I do stand up for myself now when I am talked to in a condescending tone, and I also learned that showing vulnerability makes people more open, understanding, trusting, and helpful to me. More than once, I was admired for that. There is no need to be verbally aggressive anymore. I am also not angry and sad anymore, which is an awesome feeling I want everyone to experience.

To become more flexible, I started doing yoga. Yoga made me happy with my body, helped me choose me-time more and more, and introduced me to meditation. Meditation made me feel more comfortable with myself, and mind-training audios, binaural beats, and subliminal audios did the rest. In the whole growing process, I discovered I didn't need validation and admiration so much anymore.

Because I started to believe in myself, and my life felt so much better, I decided to become a life coach. I finished my coach training, which I received from two Bob Procter trainees, and I am still working with them.

Now, I do help people through one-on-one coaching. I focus on building self-image and getting over trauma. The programs—which are available in English, Dutch and German—are designed with a bit of self-study (since changing is an inside job), audios, videos, homework, and regular meetings. Just recently, I added a program for children to the programs I offer, because I find it very important to teach children to trust and believe in themselves more. The earlier you start, the less you need to repair children and (young) adults who get damaged along the way. This is why I not only help adults but also teens and children. The children's program is for one-on-one coaching as well as perfect for schools. The programs are based on the teachings of Bob Proctor, Tony Robbins, as well as NLP and The Law of Attraction.

Nowadays, I just love learning new things, which I do on a regular basis. I read lots of nonfiction books and hardly watch TV, and I just started with energetic healing, which I hope to help my clients with soon. I also became a soul connection treatment teacher.

It is my mission to help and teach the lost ones to tap into the power within that got buried under trauma because I know it is possible and everyone deserves it.

Simone Bosman

Simone Bosman was born and raised in the Netherlands. She and her husband have two children (18 and 20), 2 cats, and a chow-chow dog. She now lives in Germany.

After 15 years working in guest-services in the Netherlands, Simone and her family moved to Germany to start their own hotel. The move was an exciting adventure to experience being entrepreneurs.

Looking back, Simone experienced several burnouts in various chapters of her life, with each time presenting a new layer of learning. Over the years, she learned to put herself first. She has grown most in areas of self-love and feeling worthy and is getting more and more confidence every day.

She finds great fulfillment in helping people overcome adversity, especially coming from (childhood) abuse, mobbing, being highly gifted and sensitive, and helps them discover their full potential. Simone approaches this using various strategies like energetic healing, reiki, and EFT. She also is passionate about health and healing through nature instead of prescription drugs. She loves making new connections and has very strong feelings about justice, especially for the vulnerable, less resilient people in society. Simone Bosman speaks Dutch, German, and English.

In her free time, Simone likes spending time with family, reading, listening to music, and doing yoga and off-road mountain biking. She now is training for her first bike-sprintrace and another bike race.

Connect with Simone at http://www.linktr.ee/petrasimonezomer.

CHAPTER 19

From a Dark Place to a Mid-life Awakening

by Suzanna Magic

Wow! Did I have a mid-life awakening! At the age of 40, I fell into a deep dark space.

Down, down, down until there was hardly any light at all. No colours. I could only see in black and white and had no energy at all. A very scary time.

One day as I was sitting on the sofa, I fell within and had the extraordinary vision of looking deep within myself. I saw my spinal column as double dotted black lines from my head to the base of my spine. At the sacral chakra, the point between my hips, I saw a huge X- the cross I had come to bear, a block I was born with.

I remember picking up and opening a book that was lying next to me. As I read the words I had the strange experience that what I was reading was the story of my life so far! A life of pleasing others rather than following my inner calling.

I didn't see anything in colour for two weeks. I was scared and lonely and sent out thoughts for help! After that I felt guided. Seeking answers, I went to a Mind Body and Spirit gathering where I went to see a healer. As he worked over my head, it felt as though he was pulling chewing gum out of my hair. I cried, asked for help. He held my hand and gave me the name and address of a healer he said could help me. I eventually looked her up and booked an appointment. On arriving at her home, the healer took my hands and said "You are what we call a sensitive-sensitive! You must have been in pain and feeling tried all your life because you are so open and feel everything."

At this point I burst into tears and said "No one has ever believed me. I've always been considered feeble, pathetic, too sensitive, too dreamy, not trying hard enough and not like others." She gave me exercises to do every day at home for a month before she could help me further. I did these exercises. They were designed to touch and release my anger and taught me how to protect my own energy by closing my chakras. At first I felt so different from my usual self, being separated from everything around me. I'd always been in pain or tired or collapsed if I couldn't cope! How odd it was to feel separate from everything! I had to get used to this new feeling of not being battered. After a month of practicing the techniques, I contacted this interesting lady again.

One evening, I was invited to sit in a psychic development circle with her. With skepticism and in trepidation, I went, desperate for answers. When I arrived for the psychic development group, I thought "Whatever am I doing here? I'm an intellectual—a scientist and a teacher. This is not for me!" However, I stayed and tentatively joined in. At one moment in the evening she gave out tarot cards, asking us to go around the circle and give a reading for someone else using the card as guidance. At this point I said, "I've no idea what you are all doing. I think it's time I went home."

With great patience, my teacher encouraged me to just have a go. I had to hold the card, decide who it related to in the circle and give a reading!

Well ... I did this and - WOW - everyone was bowled over. Apparently, I was a natural! Turns out I have a gift. A gift of being able to tune into and pick up information about people. Well, I thought everyone could do that! I'd always gone into a group of people and felt all the undercurrents, the unspoken pain, jealousy, sadness, desires, joy. I find groups and gatherings difficult because of this and am often *frozen* when in company.

I attended the psychic group regularly and I had individual healing from this lady, too. She encouraged me to *intuit* when I needed healing, rather than waiting to be told what and when I needed it. I could be my own guide and take charge of my energy! This wonderfully patient lady became my spiritual teacher, and I sat in psychic development groups for several years with her, honing my spiritual skills and learning how to use them, how to embody light and how to protect myself and my energy.

One day, my teacher phoned and asked if I was interested in learning to become a healer. "Me?" I questioned. She was running a healing class for six people and offered me a space. I said I'd think about it! A few days later, I phoned her back and said to her "You wouldn't have invited me to join this class unless you thought I could be a healer, would you?" Her reply was "I'm offering you a place, there are only six places but you have to decide for yourself if you'd like to join." I hesitated slightly, then said "YES!"

The class was so interesting and insightful, but I was always afraid and felt rather out of place.

I remembered that when I was nineteen and at university studying science, I'd been given healing for a headache by my landlord. I was very skeptical then, but it worked! He and his wife befriended me and tried to encourage me to join them at their spiritualist church. NOT FOR ME- I was far too afraid to go with them and it didn't seem to sit well with my science training!

So, many years later, I was attending healing training. I'd been called, awakened … somewhat kicking and screaming … but learning so much. After training, I worked in a healing clinic that one of the other ladies in the group had set up. I was intrigued and had many bizarre spiritual experiences. I was invited one day to attend a psychic and healing day at the clinic. I agreed to go, but as I walked in the place was packed with experienced tarot readers and healers. I felt out of my depth!

"I'll make the tea." I offered and disappeared into the kitchen. The organizer came to find me and said she needed a healer. Would I be willing to do just one. Of course, I couldn't refuse. The second client who came to me asked for a tarot reading. I felt obliged to try giving a reading. The client was delighted, and my confidence grew. I had two more delighted clients, so continued to give tarot readings. My fourth client was a gentle woman who asked for a reading. I gave her what I thought was such a beautiful reading, having had a vision of her working in a garden growing and picking flowers. I'd told her that her gift to her family was her love of the natural world. She was most upset with me, said the reading was no good and she wanted to know if her family would be successful and prosperous! I was really taken aback. I reiterated what a beautiful message this was for her, but she was not happy. I offered to arrange a reading for her with someone else and was preparing to go back into the kitchen! The very experienced guest reader came over to me and said "You have a special gift. You can read people directly; you don't really need the cards. See them as an aid and a link for you and the client. Please carry-on giving readings." I did continue and my confidence grew.

Eventually, alongside my teaching and family life, I started a meditation group of my own. I loved it and my clients loved it and found it very uplifting. One of my friends asked if I'd host a group for children. I did that too and was really delighted by how open the children were and how natural they were at supporting each other.

I qualified as a healer and I went on to train as a colour therapist, a crystal therapist, and a person-centered counsellor. It proved a great challenge to bring my spiritually aware self into the counselling course. I encountered such a lot of ego and competition and no acknowledgement of the spiritual world and soul journey.

After being contacted, out of the blue, I was asked if I'd like a job supporting children. I changed my teaching career and became a special needs support teacher. I realize now that I was being called and always have been. Looking back I realise I've never looked for a job, they have always found me. I've taught in all sorts of establishments from playgroups to high school, learning centers, homes, and cafes! I've worked with all age groups and all abilities.

My spiritual work continued alongside my teaching, and I used aspects of colour therapy, mediation, crystal therapy, counselling and teaching to be with and nurture everyone I was privileged to work with. I realized that many of the problem children I worked with actually had spiritual gifts that we talked about. When I had a conversation with them about their gifts, often they said no one had ever believed them before. The educational psychologist who visited one school I worked in came into my room one day and said "I wanted to meet you as we call you Mrs. Magic, because you change all these children and we don't know how you do it!" I have adopted this nickname, Mrs. Magic. I feel I have listened to, heard, acknowledged, and nurtured many children and adults into an understanding and acceptance of who they truly are.

I set up a bigger meditation group. It's psychic development really, but I didn't feel I could call it psychic development with my academic background. I've run groups for the last twenty-five years and used my knowledge to underpin my life and relationships, embodying divine light and working from the heart. I've learned a lot about myself, my past lives, and my unique reason for being here.

I see individual private clients and take them on their journey of awakening to being their true selves, honouring their insights and skills, learning about their past lives, releasing old patterns of behaviour. In my development groups, we have learned to support and amplify each other, develop our unique gifts and journey through the universe to gain knowledge. I teach crystal therapy one on one, adapting the curriculum to the individual skills, needs and insights of the student. I am called to be an earth healer, sending healing light to the planet, setting grids across the world, reactivating sacred sites.

What a journey of awakening I've been on. It has been quite a lonely path and I've met many challenges and obstacles, but I have always kept on going, following my visions and guidance. I've been called to take the light into many dark places.

I love this spiritual work and follow my calling to bring light, transformation, love and divine feminine energy to the planet and humanity. I have learned to embrace all my wonderful gifts and knowledge and have truly become MRS MAGIC.

I'm here to awaken others and bring understanding and divine feminine light to the planet.

Suzanna Magic

Suzanna Magic is a teacher, healer, mystic. Suzanna is mother to three wonderful children and grandmother to six precious grandchildren.

As a child, she was very sensitive and felt as though she did not really belong here. She had many weird experiences which she now understands to have been spiritual experiences. She was quiet, but knew she was wise!

Suzanna graduated with a BSc. honors degree in Biochemistry and felt a calling to teach and has taught across all age ranges. She followed an interest in complementary therapies qualifying as a Healer, Colour Therapist, Crystal Therapist, Counsellor, Play Therapist and Child Advocate. Suzanna hosts psychic development circles, teaches crystal therapy, and sees clients one on one.

Suzanna hosts Full Moon meditations online where she channels Goddess' energies and wisdom, crystal and colour energies to help bring Divine Feminine energy to earth. To follow Full Moon meditations, Suzanna is an Earth Healer and is called to sacred sites to set energy grids which re-activate power points across the planet.

Suzanna feels her soul-purpose is to foster an understanding of spirituality, nurture others on their soul journey, and bring Divine Feminine energy to earth. She writes poetry and short stories about her spiritual experiences. Suzanna's qualifications are as follows: Bachelor of Science Honors, Certification of Education, Member Healing Trust, Diploma of Colour Therapy, Diploma of Crystal Therapy, Professional Counselling, Certification Play Therapy, Child Advocacy.

Connect with Suzanna at fb.me/suzannasunflowersanctuary.com.

CHAPTER 20

Step by Step

by Tamara Fraser

I remember watching *Eat, Pray, Love* for the first time. In the movie, Liz Gilbert talks about being "an active participant in the creation of this life and yet nothing felt right." That was me every single day. I would constantly question would this ever feel right? There I was living the life I thought I was supposed to – married to an amazing man, three beautiful kids, a dog, a large home in the suburbs, jobs we both enjoyed. I had dotted all my i's and crossed all my t's and yet every single day, so much of what I was living felt so wrong. I walked around constantly rotating through a cycle of emotions. The cycle would begin with me trying to make everything feel right, which would then take me to a state of wondering when things would start to feel right. Which would then turn in to me feeling guilty for not loving all that I had. Which would then lead me to hating myself for being so ungrateful for all that I was blessed with. Then I'd go back to the beginning and try all over again.

Looking back on my life, it is easy to see now what I couldn't see then. We all know that expression that hindsight is 20/20. Now I know from deep within, that in order for me to see what I needed to see, a tremendous amount of healing had to take place. No matter what I had been told then, I needed to live the life I did in order to get to the place where I could truly awaken. One where I could live my motto, *free to be*.

After my youngest was born, I went through a phase of terrible postpartum depression and anxiety. Through my prenatal doctor, I connected with a social worker. This amazing human saw me for almost a year as we waited for me to be assigned a counsellor from the women's centre to help me continue the healing process from the sexual abuse and subsequent trauma that I had gone through as a child. She helped me process so much of what I had gone through, and she was truly pivotal in my healing journey. She taught me to separate the voice inside of my head from me and how to find my voice and what matters most to me. During my time with her, I was also connected with a psychiatrist who managed my medication and made sure I was taking care of myself and my family. I am a huge believer in all of us needing a support network and I am eternally grateful I had these humans as well as my family and friends to lean on during this tumultuous time.

It's interesting, because never during this time did it occur to me that I was gay. I believed I was living my dream and the life I was destined to. Like Gilbert, I had been an active participant in the creation of that life, so I must have wanted it. Hence, I tried. I tried to find and hold on to the happy moments. I tried to accept what I had created as mine. Yet, no matter how hard I tried, I just couldn't get to a place of peace. There was a part of me that was actively searching and the more I searched, the further it took me from the life I had created.

This part of my life, when a major part of my healing took place, is not a part of my life that I am proud of. If I could go back in time, I would. I hurt so many people and the worst part is that the people I hurt are the ones who mean the most to me. Just writing that is hard because it hurts my heart to know how much I hurt people that I care about. Though this is often the way, we tend to hurt those closest to us even if we don't intend to or want to. There are many moments I look back on with complete and utter shame and to be honest, it would be so easy to stay in that shame. I could so easily justify staying there. "Tamara, you cheated on your husband. Tamara, you lied to your family and friends. Tamara, you left your babies too often when they needed you so badly." It would be so incredibly easy to stay in the shame and relentlessly beat myself up.

I believe we are all brought to this Earth to serve others in ways that are unique to each of us. So how would my living in shame help me serve others? It wouldn't. What continues to serve others was my learning to look myself in the eyes and liking who I see. My ability to find peace with who I am is serving others because if I could do this hard thing, someone else can do their hard thing and the ripple effect of spreading light, sending strength, and creating hope, continues.

It's taken many years for me to get to this place and it's been one heck of a bumpy ride. I don't remember all the moments. I do remember some of them and those are some of the moments that feel like they helped me truly awaken. Like the first few times I kissed a girl and wondered why I liked that so much more than kissing a guy. Or the first moment I asked my oldest daughter, "What if she was more than just my friend?" and having her reply with "Like a girlfriend? Love just makes the world go 'round Mama." Or even the first moment Neal said aloud to me, "Are you really gay?" and I crumbled sobbing on the floor, nodding yes.

I'm relieved I don't remember all the moments during this time, because most days were those where I just tried to put one foot in front of the other. Over the years, I have had many people tell me they believe me to be strong and courageous. I really don't remember ever feeling that way, and to be honest, when people ask me how I made it through, I do not have an answer. I would frequently cry myself to sleep at night and wake up the next day feeling exhausted and broken. I often credit my kids when asked how I made it through. Because of them, I had to show up. Because of them, I needed to do the simple things like eat, bathe, and sleep. Because of them, I had to keep my heart open.

In life, we aren't given second chances to do things over, but we are given the chance to forgive ourselves, give ourselves the same grace we so willingly offer to others, and to choose every single day to live with integrity. Those three things have helped me accept my actions and to start liking myself. On the days when I would struggle to look in the mirror, I would ask myself, "would someone choose this hard journey?" and the answer would always be a resounding, no. I lived so much of my life feeling like something was wrong with me. Why would someone else, who felt that way, choose this path that I am now on? They wouldn't. So, I just keep moving forward one step at a time and as Glennon Doyle says, "Doing the next right thing."

I know with the utmost certainty that if I could go back and do things differently, I would. Neal deserved a wife who was honest with him. It took me a long time to refer to myself as gay and lesbian, because it took a long time to have those words feel right in my body. Not because I didn't believe them to be true, but because deep down I felt that by labelling myself, I de-valued the years I spent with him. Thoughts and questions would race around in my head like "Did I dupe him in to loving me" or "Does he know I really loved him" plaguing my mind for many years. I know that I didn't do those things. I do not believe myself capable of that level of dishonesty.

If I had known earlier on in my life, I am sure I would have chosen a different path. As time travel is not a possibility and I can't get a do-over on one of the most shame-filled times of my life, I have tried my best to honour the people I hurt in ways that show respect and gratitude. Choosing this over the reactions I sometimes wanted to choose hasn't always been easy, but it's the best way I could think of to show the special people in my life, including Neal, how much they truly do mean to me.

I don't believe I was supposed to know earlier in life though, because if I did I wouldn't have my three beautiful children. It's overwhelming to look back and see that I had so little self-worth that I believed my kids didn't need me. I recognize now that this is not at all true. Rather it was a reflection of how little I valued myself. My kids will always need me and learning to show up for them as my authentic self has been brutally hard. How could a mom who couldn't even look herself in the eyes take care of three beautiful humans? All I could do every day was take my next right step and so I did.

These steps were hard ones. I heard rumors about myself that I was scared would get back to my kids. I worried that my Zumba participants would think I was flirting with them. I was nervous that my students or their families would think less of me as a teacher. I was fearful of being able to support myself and my kids. There were so many sleepless nights and so many others where I cried myself to sleep. As with any major change in a person's life, the self-doubt voice is loud and often much crueler than it needs to be. I just chose not to listen.

I keep going – step by step – and with each step forward, I learn to like me a little more, learn to trust me a little more, and learn that I am and always will be free to be me – a gay woman with three amazing kids who loves with all of her heart and works on being her best self every single day.

Tamara Fraser

Tamara Fraser is a busy single Mama of three beautiful teenagers. She is a teacher, Zumba Instructor, Health & Fitness Coach. She loves helping busy Mamas make themselves a priority in their own lives and is on a mission to change the narrative of Moms putting everyone else first. She believes that all of us need to fill our own cups first so that we have more light and love to share with others.

Connect with Tamara at www.freetobegirls.com.

Made in the USA
Las Vegas, NV
08 June 2023

73081314R00108